Instructor's Manual
and Test Bank
to Accompany

— FOURTH EDITION —

TEN STEPS
to
IMPROVING
COLLEGE
READING SKILLS

John Langan

ATLANTIC CAPE COMMUNITY COLLEGE

Books in the Townsend Press Reading Series:

Groundwork for College Reading
Ten Steps to Building College Reading Skills
Ten Steps to Improving College Reading Skills
Ten Steps to Advancing College Reading Skills

Books in the Townsend Press Vocabulary Series:

Vocabulary Basics
Groundwork for a Better Vocabulary
Building Vocabulary Skills
Building Vocabulary Skills, Short Version
Improving Vocabulary Skills
Improving Vocabulary Skills, Short Version
Advancing Vocabulary Skills
Advancing Vocabulary Skills, Short Version
Advanced Word Power

Other Reading and Writing Books:

Everyday Heroes
English at Hand
A Basic Reader for College Writers
The Townsend Thematic Reader
Voices and Values: A Reader for Writers

Supplements Available for Most Books:

Instructor's Edition
Instructor's Manual and Test Bank
Computer Software (Windows or Macintosh)

Send book orders and requests for desk copies or supplements to:
Townsend Press Book Center
1038 Industrial Drive
West Berlin, New Jersey 08091

For even faster service, contact us in any of the following ways:
By telephone: 1-800-772-6410
By fax: 1-800-225-8894
By e-mail: townsendcs@aol.com
Through our website: www.townsendpress.com

Instructor's Manual and Test Bank to Accompany
Ten Steps to Improving College Reading Skills, Fourth Edition
ISBN 1-59194-005-2
9 8 7 6 5 4 3 2 1

CONTENTS

TEST BANKS AND ANSWERS   42

First Test Bank (Mastery Tests A–D)   43

Note: There are four mastery tests for each skill, supplementing the six mastery tests in the book itself. These tests can be used at a variety of points along the student's path of working through the chapter and the mastery tests in the book.

Second Test Bank   135

Note: These tests—two for each skill— are identical to those on the computer software available with the book. They are here mostly for reference purposes for teachers using the software tests, but they can also be copied for use in class.

NOTES FOR INSTRUCTORS

On the first three pages of the Instructor's Edition of *Ten Steps to Improving College Reading Skills*, Fourth Edition, I list some hints for teaching a reading course and for using the book. I add here some other comments.

Using a Class Contract

In the first class of the semester, I explain to students that I regard the course as a serious, professional relationship between them and me. I say that I want them to sign a professional contract for taking the course. I then pass out a contract for them to read and sign.

In my experience, the contract helps motivate younger students in particular to come to class and to assume responsibility for their own learning. Some of the older students don't need such a contract, but they welcome a clear presentation of basic ground rules regarding attendance and grading in the course.

A copy of the contract appears on pages 6–7; you have permission to modify and use this contract in whatever way you see fit.

Supplements for the Book

There are three supplements for the book:

1. An *Instructor's Edition,* which is identical to the student book except that it provides the answers to all of the practices and tests.
2. The combined *Instructor's Manual and Test Bank,* which you are now reading.
3. *Computer software,* in Windows and Macintosh formats, which contains two mastery tests for each skill plus two combined-skills tests—22 tests in all. These software tests are identical to those in the Second Test Bank in this *Instructor's Manual.* (Instructors planning to assign the software tests should **not** also give the tests in the Second Test Bank.)

If you've adopted the book for use in your reading classes, you're entitled to free copies of any of these supplements. Call 1-800-772-6410 or e-mail us at **<townsendcs@aol.com>** to get them shipped out to you immediately.

A Suggested Syllabus

Weeks 1–10:

One way to begin using the book is to have students work through the activities in "How to Become a Better Reader and Thinker" on pages 3–9. Then, as the first homework assignment, ask them to read the essay "Reading for Pleasure and Power" on pages 10–15. Discuss the questions on page 14 in the next class and urge students to take advantage of the book offer on page 15.

I suggest then teaching one chapter a week, following the order in the book. Generally at the end of a chapter I give two mastery tests: one for practice and one that counts for a grade.

I go over the tests in class right after students take them. (I recommend collecting test papers as students finish and distributing them to students in other parts of the room. Some students resist putting X's on a paper that belongs to the person sitting right next to them.) That way students get immediate feedback on how they have done. Also, after class all I need to do is to check the grades quickly and transfer them to my grade book.

As the semester progresses, I use additional mastery tests, every so often, to review previous skills covered in the class.

Weeks 11–15:

In the last five weeks, students read two selections a week from Part II of the book. They also do the remaining mastery tests, including some of the tests in this manual, as well as the combined-skills tests in the book and in this manual.

Having done all of the reading of the materials in the book, as well as all of the thinking required to complete the many activities, students are, in my experience, better readers and thinkers. They are better equipped both to handle a standardized reading test at the semester's end and to go on to content courses in their college curriculum.

Suggested Answers to the Discussion Questions

Pages 22–41 in this manual provide suggested answers to the discussion questions that follow each of the twenty readings in Parts I and II of the book. There was simply no room in the Instructor's Edition for this material.

Writing Assignments

Writing and reading are closely related skills: practice at one will make a student better at the other. Also, writing about a selection is an excellent way of thinking about it. For these reasons, two writing assignments are provided (beginning on page 585 of the book) for each of the twenty reading selections in Parts I and II.

If you ask students to write about a selection, I suggest you first have them read the "Brief Guide to Effective Writing" that appears on pages 583–584.

Teaching Vocabulary

One basic change that I've made in my teaching of reading is that I now directly teach vocabulary. We all know that students don't know enough words. Because they don't, they have trouble understanding what they read, and they're limited in what they can write. (We have all seen how, in standardized reading tests, students are frustrated because they don't know enough of the words in a passage to understand it and to answer comprehension questions about it. And we all know that because of the vocabulary problem, the standardized tests that are intended to measure reading comprehension are often in fact serving as vocabulary tests.)

I teach vocabulary using a words-in-context approach (it is of no value to ask students to memorize isolated lists of vocabulary words). Specifically, I use a book titled *Improving Vocabulary Skills, Short Version*, by Sherrie Nist and Carole Mohr. There are twenty chapters in this book, with ten words in each chapter. I do the first chapter in class, so that students understand how to use the pronunciation key for the words and understand just how the chapter works. I then assign one or two chapters a week for homework.

In class each week, I walk around and check students' books to see that they have worked through the four pages of material for each chapter. (After this quick check, I then return the focus of the class to reading skills.) Every third week, I give students one of the several tests that follow each unit of five chapters in the book. My vocabulary syllabus looks like this:

Week 2: Vocabulary chapter 1 covered in class
Week 3: Vocabulary chapters 2–3 for homework
Week 4: Vocabulary chapters 4–5 for homework plus a test on Unit One in class
Week 5: Vocabulary chapters 6–7 for homework
Week 6: Vocabulary chapters 8–9 for homework
Week 7: Vocabulary chapter 10 for homework plus a test on Unit Two in class
Week 8: Vocabulary chapters 11–12 for homework
Week 9: Vocabulary chapters 13–14 for homework
Week 10: Vocabulary chapter 15 for homework plus a test on Unit Three in class
Week 11: Vocabulary chapters 16–17 for homework
Week 12: Vocabulary chapters 18–19 for homework
Week 13: Vocabulary chapter 20 for homework plus a test on Unit Four in class

The Importance of Continual Reading and Thinking

Continual reading—coupled with thinking about what one has read—is the very heart of a reading class. *One improves the skills of reading and thinking by guided reading and thinking.* This statement is emphasized with good reason. If a teacher is not careful, he or she may play too participatory a role in the classroom, getting more reading and thinking practice than the student does. The teacher should serve as a manager, using the materials in the text to give students the skills practice they need. *Ten Steps to Improving College Reading Skills* helps the teacher ensure that students do a great deal of active reading and thinking in the classroom.

The Importance of Constant Feedback

Along with continual reading, writing, and thinking, it is vital that students get frequent feedback. Here are ways they can secure such feedback:

- Small-group interactions
- Class discussions and reviews
- Short one-on-one sessions with the teacher
- Graded quizzes and tests
- The Limited Answer Key in the back of the book
- The software tests that accompany the book
- The online exercises available at **www.townsendpress.com**

In addition, since instructors using *Ten Steps to Improving College Reading Skills* as a class text are permitted to reproduce any or all parts of this manual, you can selectively hand out copies of answers included here.

All of the exercises in the book are designed to make it easy to give clear and specific feedback. If students are going to learn to read and think more effectively, then they need clear, logical, specific responses to their efforts. This book enables teachers to provide such feedback.

Outlining, Mapping, and Summarizing

To take thoughtful, effective study notes, students need to learn three essential techniques: outlining, mapping, and summarizing. All three techniques often require students to identify the main idea and the major supporting details of a selection. But while educators agree that these three techniques are important for students to learn, they are all too seldom taught.

The book gives students instruction and practice in all three techniques. Passages in the "Supporting Details" and the two "Relationships" chapters, as well as all of the reading selections in Part II, are followed by an outline, a map, or a summary activity. To complete many of these activities, students must look closely at the basic organization of the selection. They must think carefully about what they have read by asking two key questions: "What is the point?" and "What is the support for that point?" As students apply the techniques from one selection to the next and get specific feedback on their efforts, they will develop their ability to think in a clear and logical way.

Readability Levels . . . and Their Limitations

Below are the readability grade levels for the text of the book itself and the twenty reading selections. Because the book has been prepared on a computer, and there are now software programs that determine readability, it has been possible to do a complete readability evaluation for each reading, rather than merely sampling excerpts from the materials.

Please remember, however, that there are limits to the reliability and validity of readability scores. For instance, a readability formula cannot account for such significant factors as student interest, prior knowledge of a subject, the number of examples provided to explain concepts, and the overall clarity and logic of the writing.

Thus, while "The Scholarship Jacket" has a readability level of 5th grade, it is a sophisticated adult piece that may be more challenging to students than, for example, "Students in Shock," which has a reading level of 10. And while "Child-Rearing Styles" has a readability level of 12, it is so clearly organized that it is a piece that developmental students can manage to understand. I respect readability levels, but I also take them with a grain of salt, and I have kept other factors in mind while determining the sequence of readings.

Material	Word Count	Reading Level
Text of *Ten Steps*		8
Part I		
1. Night Watch	663	7
2. Here's to Your Health	1076	9
3. Child-Rearing Styles	487	12
4. Rowing the Bus	2034	6
5. Students in Shock	1160	10
6. I Became Her Target	828	8
7. New Respect for the Nap	1139	10
8. Gender Inequality in Health Care and in the Workplace	1273	9
9. The Scholarship Jacket	1950	5
10. In Praise of the F Word	960	8

Part II

A Final Note

Writing a book that contains hundreds of explanations and activities is a bit like being in a ball game where one steps up to the batter's box an almost countless number of times. One tries to get as many hits and extra-base hits as possible: to explain every concept so that students really understand it; to provide readings and practices that both interest students and teach the skills. One tries not to hit any foul balls. Hopefully there are not too many in this Fourth Edition of a book that has benefited from a great deal of teacher and student feedback.

Realistically, though, you might find that despite my best efforts, some items may not work. If they don't, and/or if you or your students are confused or uncertain about certain items, let me know so that I can consider making changes in the next printing or revision of the book. Send a note to me at Townsend Press, 1038 Industrial Drive, West Berlin, NJ 08091. Alternatively, call Townsend Press at its toll-free number: 1-800-772-6410; send a fax to 1-800-225-8894; or send e-mail to <townsendcs@aol.com>; your comments will be passed on to me. And if you have a question, a Townsend editor will get back to you with an answer very shortly. My thanks in advance for your help in my effort to keep improving the book!

John Langan

A PROFESSIONAL CONTRACT

FOR FIFTEEN WEEKS TOGETHER

between

_____

(Student's name here)

and

_____

(Instructor's name here)

Welcome to *(name of course)* _____. Counting today, we will be spending fifteen weeks together. How successful we are will depend on how well we follow a business contract that I would like you to read and sign, and that I will then sign and return to you. Here are the terms of the contract.

MY ROLE IN THE CONTRACT

My role will be to help you practice and master important reading and writing and thinking and learning skills. I will try to present these communication skills clearly and to give you interesting and worthwhile practice materials. I will conduct this as a skills course—not a lecture course where you could borrow a friend's notes afterwards. Typically several skills will be explained briefly in class, and you will then spend most of the class time practicing those skills, making them your own. You will be learning in the best possible way: through doing.

Why learn these skills?

I promise you that the skills will be of real value to you in all the other courses you take in college. They will make you a better reader, writer, thinker, and learner, and they can dramatically increase your chance for success in school.

The skills can be just as valuable for the career work you are likely to do in the future. Consider that America is no longer an industrial society where many people work on farms or in factories. Instead, most jobs now involve providing services or processing information. More than ever, communication skills are the tools of our trade. This course will be concerned directly with helping you learn and strengthen the communication skills that will be vital for job success in the 21st century.

YOUR ROLE IN THE CONTRACT

Experiencing the course

Your role in this contract will be to come to every class and to give a full effort. Much of the value and meaning of this skills course will come from what happens in class, so you must be here on a steady basis. Imagine trying to learn another skill without being present: for example, imagine learning how to drive without the *experience* of actually being in the car and working with the controls and getting feedback from your instructor. How much would you learn about the skill of driving if you relied only on the notes of a classmate? In a similar way, to really learn communication skills, you need direct experience and practice. So if you miss classes, you are in effect missing the course.

6

Shaping your attitude

Some people start college with a "high-school mindset." They are passive; they do the minimum they need to get by; their attention is elsewhere; they are like the living dead—and the American high-school system (and watching thousands of hours of television) may be to blame. Gradually these people realize that college is not high school: they don't have to be in college, and they are no longer part of the sad game played out in many high schools, where they receive a free ride and promotion no matter how little they do.

If your attitude about learning has been hurt by what happened in high school, then part of your role is to change your attitude. You can do so, and this contract will help.

Understanding sick days and personal days

You should try not to miss *any* classes. But in the professional environment of this class, like in the work world, everyone is entitled to a set number of sick days as well as "personal days"—unexplained absences. In this course, you will have a total of *(insert number)* _____ such days—which can cover such real-world happenings as sickness, car breakdowns, or even the death of someone you know. If you missed more than this amount of time in a real-world job contract, you would be let go. (Only in some extraordinary situation, such as an extended illness confirmed by a doctor's report, might an exception apply.) The professional terms of the work world will apply here: if you miss more than _____ classes, you cannot pass the course.

YOUR ROLE IF YOU MISS CLASS

If you do miss a class, you are responsible for getting the homework for the following week's class. To do so, call a classmate. Write down the names and phone numbers of two people in the room. (For now, use the people sitting on either side of you; you can always change these names later.)

Classmate # 1: *Name* _____   *Phone* _____

Classmate # 2: *Name* _____   *Phone* _____

Note that you **must** turn in all homework assignments or you **cannot pass the course**.

If a test or tests are given on a day you miss class, you cannot ordinarily make up these tests. Instead, you will receive a grade of M (Missing) for each missed test. When all your grades are averaged at the end of the semester, three M's will be omitted; the rest will convert to zeros.

YOUR COMMITMENT

I've read this contract, and the terms seem fair to me. (I like the fact that this college class is being treated as a professional situation, and I'm learning the ground rules up front.) I accept the responsibility and the challenge to make this course worth my time and money.

_____   _____

Signed by (your name here)   *Date*

_____

Witnessed by the instructor

OR: If you don't want to sign this, please meet with me after this class to talk about why.

ANSWERS TO THE TESTS IN THE BOOK

Answers to the Review and Mastery Tests in Part I

VOCABULARY IN CONTEXT:
Review Test 1

1. context
2. A
3. C
4. B
5. definition . . . examples

VOCABULARY IN CONTEXT:
Review Test 2

A. 1. B
2. A
3. B
4. C
5. A

B. 6. D overjoyed
7. A provided
8. C discouraged
9. E nag
10. B doubtful

VOCABULARY IN CONTEXT:
Review Test 3

A. 1. practical
2. clean
3. reveal
4. relieve
5. at the same time

B. 6. looked down upon
7. guilty
8. tried
9. add to
10. joined

VOCABULARY IN CONTEXT:
Review Test 4

1. B
2. D
3. D
4. B
5. A
6. A
7. C
8. D
9. D
10. C

VOCABULARY IN CONTEXT:
Mastery Test 1

A. 1. D
2. B
3. C
B. 4. risk
5. search
6. false name
C. 7. C
8. B
9. A
10. B

VOCABULARY IN CONTEXT:
Mastery Test 2

A. 1. B
2. A
3. plain
4. conduct
5. modest
B. 6. C
7. C
8. D
9. D
10. B

VOCABULARY IN CONTEXT:
Mastery Test 3

1. A
2. C
3. C
4. C
5. B
6. D
7. D
8. C
9. A
10. B

VOCABULARY IN CONTEXT:
Mastery Test 4

1. C
2. C
3. A
4. B
5. D
6. C
7. A
8. D
9. B
10. C

VOCABULARY IN CONTEXT:
Mastery Test 5

A. 1. C
2. D
3. C
4. A
5. C

B. *(Wording of answers may vary.)*
6. cut off
7. give a false account of; misrepresent; twist
8. come between; get involved
9. required
10. became more forgiving; gave in

VOCABULARY IN CONTEXT:
Mastery Test 6

A. 1. E most common
2. C stir up interest
3. F uncontrolled
4. I increased
5. B passed

B. 6. I die
7. D deadly
8. F be forced to experience
9. E give credit for
10. J reducing

MAIN IDEAS:
Review Test 1

1. B 4. A
2. B 5. other sentences
3. A in the paragraph

MAIN IDEAS:
Review Test 2

A. 1. a. S   B. 1. a. SD
   b. S   b. SD
   c. S   c. T
   d. P   d. MI
   2. a. S   2. a. SD
   b. S   b. SD
   c. P   c. T
   d. S   d. MI

MAIN IDEAS:
Review Test 3

1. 3
2. 1
3. 9
4. 2
5. 2

MAIN IDEAS:
Review Test 4

1. D   6. C
2. C   7. A
3. A   8. D
4. A   9. A
5. C   10. A

MAIN IDEAS:
Mastery Test 1

A. 1. a. S   B. 1. a. SD
   b. P   b. T
   c. S   c. SD
   d. S   d. MI
   2. a. P   2. a. MI
   b. S   b. SD
   c. S   c. T
   d. S   d. SD
   3. a. S
   b. S
   c. S
   d. P

MAIN IDEAS:
Mastery Test 2

A. 1. a. S   B. 1. a. SD
   b. P   b. SD
   c. S   c. T
   d. S   d. MI
   2. a. S   2. a. MI
   b. S   b. T
   c. P   c. SD
   d. S   d. SD
   3. a. P
   b. S
   c. S
   d. S

MAIN IDEAS:
Mastery Test 3

1. 1
2. 2
3. 6
4. 1
5. 2

MAIN IDEAS:
Mastery Test 4

1. 3
2. 2
3. 1
4. 7
5. 2

MAIN IDEAS:
Mastery Test 5

1. 6
2. 4
3. 2
4. 1
5. 2

MAIN IDEAS:
Mastery Test 6

1. 2
2. 1
3. 2
4. 3
5. 11

SUPPORTING DETAILS:
Review Test 1

1. specific . . . specific
2. T
3. supporting details
4. mapping
5. condense

SUPPORTING DETAILS:
Review Test 2

A. *Main idea:* Several factors influence the justice system's treatment of criminals.
  1. Sex of offender affects severity of sentence
    b. Court more reluctant to send mother to prison than father
  2. Race is another factor
    a. Nonwhites awarded parole and probation less often
    b. Blacks executed more often for capital crimes
  3. a. Young offenders given special treatment
B. 8. C   9. C   10. B

SUPPORTING DETAILS:
Review Test 3

A. *Main idea:* Serious depression has definite warning signs.
  1. Change in sleep patterns
  2. Abnormal eating patterns
  3. Trouble in thinking or concentrating
  4. General feeling of hopelessness
B. *Main idea:* There are three common ways that people deal with their feelings.

Withhold them   Display them   Describe them

C. 10. C

(In all these tests, wording of main ideas and supporting details may vary.)

SUPPORTING DETAILS:
Review Test 4

1. B
2. A
3. D
4. A
5. long interviews
6–10. A. 1. Basic temperament the child is born with
      2. Early emotional environment
    B. 1. Authoritative
      2. Authoritarian
      3. Permissive

SUPPORTING DETAILS:
Mastery Test 1

A. *Main idea:* Divorce has serious negative consequences.
  1. a. Starting to date again can be nerve-racking.
  2. Emotional difficulties among original family members are common.
    a. Husband and wife feel guilt and resentment.
  3. Financial adjustments are necessary.
    a. Alimony, child support, and property disposal must be dealt with.
B. 7. B   8. A   9. C
  10. They can undo complicated bolts on gates.

SUPPORTING DETAILS:
Mastery Test 2

A. 1. B   4. D
    2. D   5. C
    3. C   6. B

B. *Main idea:* Chimpanzees use objects in their environment as tools.
  1. Sticks to catch termites and steal honey
  2. Leaves as drinking cups, for cleaning, and as sponges
  3. Stones to crack open nuts

(In all these tests, wording of main ideas and supporting details may vary.)

SUPPORTING DETAILS:
Mastery Test 3

A. 1. A   4. D
    2. B   5. B
    3. A   6. A

B. *Main idea:* Three types of human memory allow us to remove or keep information as needed.
  1. Sensory memory
  2. Short-term memory—stores about 7 items for about 30 seconds.
  3. Long-term memory—stores enormous numbers of items for a long period.

SUPPORTING DETAILS:
Mastery Test 4

A. *Main idea:* Researchers have created a number of theories to explain the functions of sleep.
  1. Gives body time to repair brain cells and create chemical that makes brain think
  2. Enables body to save energy
  3. Keeps people out of trouble
  4. Reduces memory
B. 6. C
C. 7. A
    8. B
    9. B
    10. D

SUPPORTING DETAILS:
Mastery Test 5

A. 1. B   4. B
    2. D   5. C
    3. A

B. *Main idea:* Experts in our country have suggested various purposes of imprisonment.

Punish-ment   Rehabil-itation   Deter crime   Keep criminals off streets

SUPPORTING DETAILS:
Mastery Test 6

A. 1. a. 2) Informal and friendly atmosphere in the Senate
      b. Procedural differences
        1) House rules—many and complex
        2) Senate rules—short and simple
  3. Political outlook of members
    a. Representatives concerned with local issues
B. *Main idea:* A number of conditions stimulate aggression.

Pain   Attacks   Crowding

IMPLIED MAIN IDEAS AND THE CENTRAL POINT:
Review Test 1
1. implied
2. topic
3. support
4. central point
5. sometimes

IMPLIED MAIN IDEAS AND THE CENTRAL POINT:
Review Test 2
1. B
2. A
3. Watching TV has several benefits.
4. Lower-class criminals tend to be treated more harshly by the justice system than higher-class criminals.

(In all these tests, wording of implied main ideas may vary.)

IMPLIED MAIN IDEAS AND THE CENTRAL POINT:
Review Test 3
1. B
2. D
3. Several techniques can help you get a good night's sleep.
4. Sentence 2

IMPLIED MAIN IDEAS AND THE CENTRAL POINT:
Review Test 4
1. B
2. C
3. A
4. A
5. D
6. A
7. C
8. A
9. D
10. B

IMPLIED MAIN IDEAS AND THE CENTRAL POINT:
Mastery Test 1
A. 1. C
2. A
3. D
B. 4. Sentence 1

IMPLIED MAIN IDEAS AND THE CENTRAL POINT:
Mastery Test 2
A. 1. C
2. B
3. D
B. 4. Sentence 20

IMPLIED MAIN IDEAS AND THE CENTRAL POINT:
Mastery Test 3
A. 1. A
2. A
3. D
B. 4. Sentence 19

IMPLIED MAIN IDEAS AND THE CENTRAL POINT:
Mastery Test 4
A. 1. D
2. B
B. 3. There are several positive ways to encourage your family to exercise more often.
C. 4. Sentence 16

IMPLIED MAIN IDEAS AND THE CENTRAL POINT:
Mastery Test 5
A. 1. D
2. D
B. 3. Experts have suggested several techniques for doing well on exams.
C. 4. Sentence 3

IMPLIED MAIN IDEAS AND THE CENTRAL POINT:
Mastery Test 6
A. 1. D
2. B
B. 3. Marriage is good for people's physical and mental health.
C. 4. Sentence 10

RELATIONSHIPS I:
Review Test 1
1. the relationships between
2. addition
3. time
4. T
5. supporting details

RELATIONSHIPS I:
Review Test 2
A. 1. E before
   2. C also
   3. D one
   4. A then
   5. F final
6. B second
B. 7. B
   8. after
   9. A
   10. also

RELATIONSHIPS I:
Review Test 3
A. 1. After
   2. First
   3. Then
   4. As
   5. later
6. B
B. 7. B
   8. A
   9. B
   10. A

(In all these tests, wording of main ideas and supporting details may vary.)

RELATIONSHIPS I:
Review Test 4
1. B
2. D
3. B
4. A
5. A
6. C
7. first
   another
   final
8. A
9. finally
10. B

RELATIONSHIPS I:
Mastery Test 1
A. 1. A Another
   2. E When
   3. C also
   4. B Then
   5. D Next
B. 6. after
   7. next
   8. Last
   9. then
   10. B

RELATIONSHIPS I:
Mastery Test 2
A. 1. A When
   2. D First
   3. B Moreover
   4. C Before
   5. E also
B. 6. B
C. 7. First
   8. also
   9. Finally
   10. A

RELATIONSHIPS I:
Mastery Test 3
A. 1–5. 3, 1, 4, 2, A
B.   6. B
C.   7. A
8–10. *Main idea:* Prevention against injury involves a combination of two types of preventive measures.
   1. Active prevention—methods that require people to do something to reduce the risk of injury.
   2. Passive prevention—methods requiring little or no action on the part of those being protected.

RELATIONSHIPS I:
Mastery Test 4
A. 1–4. 4, 1, 3, 2
   5. B
B.   6. B
C. *Main idea:* Work shapes human lives in fundamental ways.

Consumes enormous amounts of time   Gives life structure and rhythm   Causes stress

RELATIONSHIPS I:
Mastery Test 5
A. 1. B
   2. early (*or* later *or* eventually *or* next)
B. 3. A
   4. C
C. 5. B
6–10.

Acceptance   Denial

Bargaining   Anger

Depression

RELATIONSHIPS I:
Mastery Test 6
A. 1. B
2–3. *Any two of the following:* first, next, third, finally
B. 4. A
   5. also
   6. A
C. 7. A
8–10. *Main idea:* Children learn their gender roles in three main ways.
   2. Imitation
   3. Self-definition

RELATIONSHIPS II:
Review Test 1
1. examples   4. C
2. comparison   5. C
3. contrast

RELATIONSHIPS II:
Review Test 2
A. 1. B effects   B.   6. B
    2. C just like   7. C
    3. E However   8. A
    4. A Because   9. C
    5. D such as   10. A

RELATIONSHIPS II:
Mastery Test 1
A. 1. B For example   B. 6. A
    2. C Just as   7. C
    3. A Therefore   8. A
    4. D Because   9. B
    5. E In contrast   10. C

RELATIONSHIPS II:
Mastery Test 4
A. 1–4. 4, 1, 3, 2
    5. A
B. 6. A
    7. B
    8. as the result
C. 9. B
    10. C

(In Tests 5 and 6, wording of main ideas and supporting details may vary.)

RELATIONSHIPS I and II:
Mastery Test 1
A. 1. B Then   B. 6. D However
    2. C for example   7. C After
    3. D First   8. E As a result
    4. E cause   9. A For instance
    5. A unlike   10. B next

RELATIONSHIPS II:
Review Test 3
A. 1. A
    2. for instance
B. 3. C
    4. alike *or* but *or* while *or* in contrast
C. 5. B
    6. because *or* as a result *or* effect
D. 7. A
    8. example
E. 9. B
    10. affected *or* because *or* result

RELATIONSHIPS II:
Mastery Test 2
A. 1. B
    2. reason *or* as a result
B. 3. C
    4. in contrast
C. 5. A
    6. for example
D. 7. B
    8. causing *or* since *or* leads to *or* causes
E. 9. C
    10. different *or* contrasts *or* nevertheless *or* same *or* alike *or* similar

RELATIONSHIPS II:
Mastery Test 5
A. 1. B
    2–5. Learn to do their jobs better
         Get a raise or promotion
         Learn a new field
         Learn for the sake of learning
B. 6. B
    7–10. *Good manager*
         4. Is flexible
         Poor manager
         1. Is surprised by problems
         3. Takes on extra tasks
         4. Clings to old rules

RELATIONSHIIPS I and II:
Mastery Test 2
A. 1. C
    2. different *or* however
B. 3. C
    4. reason *or* due to *or* causes
C. 5. B
    6. for instance *or* example
D. 7. A
    8. when *or* then *or* as *or* now *or* after
E. 9. B
    10. one *or* another *or* third

RELATIONSHIPS II:
Review Test 4
1. B   6. B
2. C   7. C
3. C   8. A
4. B   9. B
5. A   10. D

RELATIONSHIPS II:
Mastery Test 3
A. 1–4. 3, 2, 4, 1
    5. C
B. 6. C
    7. differently *or* in contrast *or* while
C. 8. D
    9. A
    10. example

RELATIONSHIPS II:
Mastery Test 6
A. 1. C
    2–6. Delays
         Lack of resources
         Losses
         Failure
         Discrimination
B. 7. B
    8–10. *Main idea:* Role conflict—a situation in which the different roles an individual is expected to play make incompatible demands.

For a working mother, the expectations of motherhood may conflict with those of a full-time job.

For a priest, the responsibility to treat confessions confidentially may conflict with his responsibility to the community.

RELATIONSHIPS I and II:
Mastery Test 3
A. 1. C
B. 2. B
C. 3. A
D. 4. A
E. 5. B

FACT AND OPINION:
Review Test 1
1. A fact
2. A news report
3. a mixture of fact and opinion
4. Opinions
5. enjoyable

FACT AND OPINION:
Review Test 2
A. 1. F
2. O
3. F
4. O
B. 5. F+O
6. F+O
7. F
8. F+O
C. 9. F
10. F+O

FACT AND OPINION:
Review Test 3
A. 1. O
2. F
3. F+O
4. F
5. F+O
6. O
7. F
8. F
9. O
10. F+O

B. 1. 1. F+O
2. F
3. O
4. F
5. O
2. 1. O
2. F
3. F
4. F+O
5. O

FACT AND OPINION:
Review Test 4
1. D
2. B
3. D
4. C
5. C
6. D
7. short naps
8. C
9. A
10. A

FACT AND OPINION:
Mastery Test 1
A. 1. F
2. O
3. F
4. O
5. O
6. F
7. F
8. O
9. F
10. O
B. 11. F+O
12. F
13. F+O
14. F
15. F+O
C. 1. F
2. F+O
3. F
4. O
5. O

FACT AND OPINION:
Mastery Test 2
A. 1. O
2. F
3. O
4. F
5. F
6. O
7. O
8. F
9. O
10. F
B. 11. F+O
12. F
13. F+O
14. F+O
15. F
C. 1. F
2. F+O
3. F
4. O
5. O

FACT AND OPINION:
Mastery Test 3
A. 1. F
2. O
3. F
4. F+O
5. O
6. F
7. F
8. O
9. F
10. F+O
B. 11. F+O
12. F
13. F+O
14. F
15. F+O
C. 1. O
2. F
3. F
4. F+O
5. O

FACT AND OPINION:
Mastery Test 4
A. 1. O
2. F+O
3. O
4. O
5. F
6. F+O
7. F
8. F
9. F
10. F
11. F
12. O
B. 1. F+O
2. O
3. F
4. F
5. F
C. 18. F
19. F+O
20. O

FACT AND OPINION:
Mastery Test 5
A. 1. O
2. F
3. F+O
4. O
5. F
6. F
7. O
8. F
9. F
10. F
11. O
12. F+O
B. 1. O
2. F+O
3. F
4. F
5. F
C. 16. F+O
17. F
18. F
19. O
20. F+O

FACT AND OPINION:
Mastery Test 6
A. 1. F
2. F
3. O
4. F
5. F+O
6. F
7. F
8. O
9. F+O
10. O
B. 1. F
2. F
3. F+O
4. F
5. F+O
C. 16. F
17. F
18. F+O
19. O
20. F

ERRATA:

1. On page 260 of the text, the first paragraph should read as follows: Elizabeth L. Miller was born on December 4, 1823, and died on July 21, 1889. She was the wife of H.R. Miller.

2. On page 293, the directions for Part B should read: Note that **two** sentences combine fact and opinion.

These errors will be corrected in the second printing of the book.

INFERENCES:
Review Test 1
1. suggested 4. T
2. useful 5. tell . . . show
3. useful

INFERENCES:
Review Test 2
A. 1, 3, 5, 7
B. 2, 4, 6, 7
C. 1, 2

INFERENCES:
Review Test 3
A. 1, 3, 5, 6
B. 5. A 8. A
6. A 9. A
7. B 10. C

INFERENCES:
Review Test 4
1. B 6. A
2. D 7. B
3. C 8. D
4. C 9. D
5. A 10. B

INFERENCES:
Mastery Test 1
A. 1, 4, 6
B. 2, 3, 4
C. 1. 2, 5
2. 1, 5

INFERENCES:
Mastery Test 2
A. 1. C 3. A
2. B 4. C
B. 2, 4, 5, 6, 8, 10

INFERENCES:
Mastery Test 3
A. 1. A 3. C
2. B 4. A
B. 4, 5
C. 1, 3, 5, 8

INFERENCES:
Mastery Test 4
A. 1. C B. 6. A
2. C 7. A
3. C 8. C
4. B 9. B
5. A 10. B

INFERENCES:
Mastery Test 5
A. 2, 3, 5, 6
B. 5. A
6. B
7. C
8. C
9. A
10. B

INFERENCES:
Mastery Test 6
A. 1. C B. 6. B
2. B 7. A
3. B 8. C
4. C 9. A
5. A 10. A

15

PURPOSE AND TONE:
Review Test 1

1. purpose	6. opposite
2. inform	7. B
3. entertain	8. C
4. persuade	9. C
5. attitude	10. B

PURPOSE AND TONE:
Review Test 2

1. P	4. I
2. I	5. P
3. E	

PURPOSE AND TONE:
Review Test 3

1. C
2. E
3. B
4. D
5. H

PURPOSE AND TONE:
Review Test 4

1. D	6. B
2. C	7. B
3. B	8. B
4. A	9. A
5. D	10. C

PURPOSE AND TONE:
Mastery Test 1

A.	1. I	B.	6. D
	2. P		7. B
	3. E		8. E
	4. P		9. C
	5. E		10. A

PURPOSE AND TONE:
Mastery Test 2

A.	1. I		6. I
	2. P		7. P
	3. E	B.	8. C
	4. I		9. E
	5. P		10. A

PURPOSE AND TONE:
Mastery Test 3

A.	1. B		6. J
	2. H		7. C
	3. F	B.	8. I
	4. I		9. P
	5. D		10. E

PURPOSE AND TONE:
Mastery Test 4

A.	1. E		6. F
	2. A		7. J
	3. I	B.	8. I
	4. C	C.	9. C
	5. G		10. B

PURPOSE AND TONE:
Mastery Test 5

A.	1. B	C.	5. B
	2. C		6. D
B	3. A	D.	7. C
	4. D		8. D

PURPOSE AND TONE:
Mastery Test 6

A.	1. A	C.	5. B
	2. A		6. A
B	3. A	D.	7. A
	4. B		8. D

ARGUMENT:
Review Test 1
- 1. C   4. B
- 2. A   5. D
- 3. C

ARGUMENT:
Review Test 2
- A. 1. B   B. 5. B
- 2. B   6. D
- 3. D   7. E
- 4. C   8. A
-               9. D
-               10. F

ARGUMENT:
Review Test 3
- A. 1. C
- 2. A
- 3. D
- B. 4. D
- 5. C

ARGUMENT:
Review Test 4
- 1. C   6. A
- 2. D   7. A
- 3. C   8. C
- 4. C   9. B
- 5. D   10. A. S
-               B. P
-               C. X
-               D. S

ARGUMENT:
Mastery Test 1
- A. 1. A   B. 5. A
- 2. D   6. D
- 3. B   7. E
- 4. A   8. B
-               9. D
-               10. E

ARGUMENT:
Mastery Test 2
- A. 1. C   7. A
- 2. C   8. C
- 3. B   9. F
- B. 4. A   C. 10. D
- 5. D
- 6. E

ARGUMENT:
Mastery Test 3
- A. 1. C   B. 4. D
- 2. B   5. B
- 3. D

ARGUMENT:
Mastery Test 4
- A. 1. A   B. 4. C
- 2. D   5. D
- 3. A

ARGUMENT:
Mastery Test 5
- A. 1. A   B. 7. C
- 2. D   C. 8. A
- 3. F   C. 9. B
- 4. B   10. B
- 5. C
- 6. F

ARGUMENT:
Mastery Test 6
- A. 1. B   B. 7. C
- 2. D   C. 8. A
- 3. F   C. 9. B
- 4. B   10. A
- 5. C
- 6. F

Answers to the Reading Selections in Part II

1 THE YELLOW RIBBON

Skills Questions

1. A	6. B	11. D	16. C
2. B	7. D	12. C	17. C
3. D	8. B	13. C	18. C
4. B	9. C	14. B	19. A
5. F	10. D	15. T	20. C

Summarizing

B

2 URBAN LEGENDS

Skills Questions

1. D	6. D	11. A	16. D
2. A	7. A	12. A	17. A
3. D	8. B	13. A	18. B
4. C	9. C	14. C	19. C
5. A	10. D	15. B	20. B

Mapping

What they are

Gather more realistic details and variations as they travel

The playboy's car

The cement-truck driver's revenge

3 SHAME

Skills Questions

1. C	6. T	11. B	16. T
2. D	7. B	12. B	17. T
3. C	8. C	13. B	18. D
4. A	9. D	14. F	19. T
5. D	10. C	15. C	20. A

Outlining

1. Becomes ashamed of his poverty
   b. Is humiliated by teacher
   c. Leaves school and avoids it in the future
2. Becomes ashamed of his own failure to help another
   c. Offers to pay for meal, but too late

4 THE BYSTANDER EFFECT

Skills Questions

1. C	6. D	11. A	16. D
2. D	7. C	12. D	17. B
3. B	8. D	13. D	18. C
4. D	9. C	14. A	19. C
5. D	10. D	15. C	20. B

Summarizing *(Note: Wording of answers may vary.)*

witnesses present

no one called the police during the attack

the reactions of bystanders to emergencies

interpret

is felt by each member of the crowd

5 THE REAL STORY OF FLIGHT 93

Skills Questions

1. D	6. C	11. B	16. D
2. B	7. A	12. A	17. A
3. B	8. A	13. B	18. C
4. A	9. D	14. D	19. B
5. F	10. C	15. D	20. D

Outlining

1. Introduction—paragraphs 1 to 4
   a. Lisa Beamer's conversations with counselor and Airfone supervisor
2. Narrative of the events of Flight 93— paragraphs 5 to 31
3. Conclusion—paragraphs 32 to 33
   a. Lisa Beamer as hero's widow
   b. Teddy Roosevelt's words

6 COPING WITH NERVOUSNESS

Skills Questions

1. C	6. C	11. A	16. D
2. B	7. B	12. A	17. D
3. B	8. C	13. A	18. C
4. A	9. B	14. A	19. A
5. C	10. D	15. A	20. A

Outlining

B. People can learn to cope with the fear of public speaking.
C. There are various ways to cope with your nervousness about public speaking.
   2. Prepare adequately for your speech.
   4. Use coping methods for walking to the speaker's stand and just after.

7 COMPLIANCE TECHNIQUES

Skills Questions

1. C	6. C	11. C	16. B
2. D	7. D	12. D	17. D
3. A	8. D	13. C	18. F
4. A	9. C	14. A	19. B
5. B	10. A	15. C	20. C

Summarizing *(Note: Wording of answers may vary.)*

2. . . . making a smaller request. The first request is so outrageously large that people might be tempted to slam the door in the requester's face.
   Example: . . . to give a great deal of time.

3. asking a person to agree to something on the basis of incomplete information and then later telling the full story.

4. *Example:* At a bake sale, customers were more likely to buy cupcakes for 75 cents if they were told they would also get two free cookies.

8 LIZZIE BORDEN

Skills Questions

1. C	6. A	11. B	16. C
2. C	7. C	12. A	17. A
3. C	8. D	13. A	18. B
4. A	9. B	14. C	19. D
5. B	10. C	15. C	20. B

Summarizing

B

9 NONVERBAL COMMUNICATION

Skills Questions

1. B	6. A	11. C	16. A
2. B	7. D	12. B	17. B
3. C	8. B	13. A	18. A
4. D	9. D	14. T	19. B
5. A	10. C	15. B	20. D

Outlining *(Note: Wording of answers may vary.)*

A. Nonverbal messages: the use of personal space
   3. Social distance
   4. Public distance
B. 2. a. Helps communicate certain emotions, attitudes, and preferences
      b. Supports our verbal communications

10 PREINDUSTRIAL CITIES

Skills Questions

1. C	6. B	11. C	16. A
2. B	7. T	12. A	17. A
3. B	8. C	13. B	18. D
4. B	9. A	14. B	19. B
5. A	10. C	15. D	20. Preindustrial cities were more crowded (*or* dangerous *or* disease-ridden).

Mapping

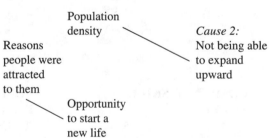

Disease limited size of city

Population density

Reasons people were attracted to them

Cause 2: Not being able to expand upward

Opportunity to start a new life

Answers to the Tests in Part III

COMBINED SKILLS:
Test 1

1. C   5. B
2. C   6. C
3. A   7. D
4. A   8. D

COMBINED SKILLS:
Test 2

1. B   5. A
2. D   6. B
3. B   7. A
4. B   8. C

COMBINED SKILLS:
Test 3

1. B   5. D
2. D   6. A
3. C   7. B
4. B   8. A

COMBINED SKILLS:
Test 4

1. B   5. A
2. B   6. C
3. A   7. A
4. C   8. D

COMBINED SKILLS:
Test 5

1. B   5. B
2. C   6. D
3. C   7. C
4. D   8. B

COMBINED SKILLS:
Test 6

1. D   5. B
2. A   6. A
3. A   7. A
4. B   8. C

COMBINED SKILLS:
Test 7

1. B   5. D
2. A   6. B
3. D   7. C
4. C   8. D

COMBINED SKILLS:
Test 8

1. D   5. C
2. D   6. A
3. B   7. D
4. D   8. C

COMBINED SKILLS:
Test 9

1. A   5. C
2. B   6. B
3. B   7. C
4. D   8. B

COMBINED SKILLS:
Test 10

1. C   5. C
2. C   6. C
3. B   7. D
4. B   8. D

COMBINED SKILLS:
Test 11

1. C   5. A
2. D   6. B
3. C   7. A
4. C   8. C

COMBINED SKILLS:
Test 12

1. C   5. C
2. B   6. A
3. C   7. C
4. A   8. B

COMBINED SKILLS:
Test 13

1. C   5. B
2. B   6. A
3. A   7. D
4. C   8. B

COMBINED SKILLS:
Test 14

1. B   5. A
2. D   6. A
3. A   7. B
4. C   8. A

COMBINED SKILLS:
Test 15

1. A   5. A
2. C   6. D
3. A   7. C
4. C   8. A

PROPAGANDA:
Review Test 1
1. B
2. A
3. A
4. A
5. B

PROPAGANDA:
Review Test 2
1. D   6. C
2. A   7. B
3. A   8. D
4. D   9. A
5. C   10. A

PROPAGANDA:
Review Test 3
A. 1. B   6. B
2. D   7. A
3. C   8. D
4. C   B. 9. B
5. C   10. C

PROPAGANDA:
Mastery Test 1
1. A   6. C
2. D   7. A
3. A   8. D
4. B   9. D
5. C   10. A

PROPAGANDA:
Mastery Test 2
A. 1. D   6. C
2. B   7. A
3. D   8. B
4. D   B. 9. B
5. B   10. C

PROPAGANDA:
Mastery Test 3
A. 1. B   C. 6. B
2. A   7. B
B. 3. D   8. C
4. B   D. 9. A
5. B   10. C

PROPAGANDA:
Mastery Test 4
A. 1. C   C. 6. B
2. C   7. C
B. 3. D   D. 8. D
4. C   9. C
5. B   10. A

PROPAGANDA:
Mastery Test 5
A. 1. C   6. E
2. B   7. C
3. F   8. D
4. D   B. 9. B
5. A   10. B

PROPAGANDA:
Mastery Test 6
A. 1. B   6. A
2. D   7. B
3. C   8. C
4. E   B. 9. A
5. F   10. C

MORE ABOUT ARGUMENT:
Review Test 1
1. T
2. T
3. F
4. C
5. B

MORE ABOUT ARGUMENT:
Review Test 2
A. 1. C   B. 6. A
2. B   7. C
3. A   8. B
4. C   9. C
5. A   10. A

MORE ABOUT ARGUMENT:
Review Test 3
A. 1. B   B. 6. A
2. A   7. C
3. C   8. B
4. B   9. A
5. A   10. B

SUGGESTED ANSWERS TO THE DISCUSSION QUESTIONS IN PART I

Note: The numbers in parentheses refer to paragraphs in the reading. For some questions, additional related questions have been included to enhance class discussion.

1   NIGHT WATCH, Roy Popkin

1. *When do you think the Marine realized that calling him to the hospital was a mistake? Was it when he first saw the old man or before? What parts of the reading support your conclusion?*

   The Marine's comment in paragraph 13 suggests that he knew there had been a mistake when he first saw the old man: "I knew right off there'd been a mistake, but I also knew he needed his son." This is stated as though he made the judgment at the hospital, upon seeing the man and perhaps realizing that nobody else was there to be with him as he died.

2. *How do you think the dead man's real son felt about the other Marine being with his dying father? How would you feel?*

   Many readers will feel that the real son would have mixed feelings—great gratitude for the Marine's kindness, jealousy of a stranger who spent crucial time with his father, and sadness at having been denied the opportunity to be with his father one more time.

3. *The incident in the reading took place because of some surprising coincidences. What were they? Has a surprising or interesting coincidence ever taken place in your life? If so, what was it, and how did it affect you?*

   The coincidences in the reading were "there had been two Marines with the same name and similar serial numbers in the camp" (14). Answers will vary.

4. *By going out of his way for a stranger, the Marine showed "in a uniquely human way that there are people who care what happens to others." Have you ever gone out of your way to help a stranger? Or have you seen someone else do so? Tell what the situation was and what happened.*

   Answers will vary.

2 HERE'S TO YOUR HEALTH, Joan Dunayer

1. *Unfortunately, Tod's experience with alcohol is not so rare. Do you know anyone who has had a negative experience because of drinking or because of drinking and driving? Where was that person drinking, and how much did he or she have? Explain what eventually happened.*

   Answers will vary. (Students may also be able to draw upon the local news for stories of drinking and driving.)

2. *If it's true that "beer doesn't make anyone sexier," why do you think so many young people drink so much beer in social situations?*

   One important reason is that alcohol lowers inhibitions, giving young people the confidence they seek to relax among others and reach out for social connections, both romantic and otherwise. Another reason, of course, is that young people tend to feel peer pressure and thus behave as their peers do; if some in a group are drinking, others are likely to do so as well.

3. *Think about a wine, liquor, or beer ad you have seen in a magazine, in a newspaper, or on television. What part of the alcohol myth described in "Here's to Your Health" does that ad promote? What details of the ad contribute to that element of the myth?*

   Students can discuss current ads on TV and in campus publications. Inevitably, all alcohol ads include some element of the myth, perhaps most commonly the idea that alcohol makes one attractive to the opposite sex. Bringing magazine ads to class may enliven discussion on this question.

4. *Cigarette advertising is no longer allowed on television. Do you think beer ads should also be outlawed on TV? In college newspapers? Explain your answers.*

   Answers will vary, but students can address such issues as the causes and effects of drunk driving and the results of extensive student drinking, as well as alcohol companies' rights of expression.

3   CHILD-REARING STYLES, Diane E. Papalia and Sally Wendkos Olds

1. *What type of parenting style did you grow up with? Would you say this style was effective? Why or why not?*

To answer this question, students can look back at the specific elements of each type of parenting and think of examples from their own upbringing that fit a particular description. For instance, a student who states that his parents "set few rules" (permissive parents, 5) might tell about some behaviors that were allowed in his or her home that are unlikely to be allowed in other homes. Answers to the second and third questions will vary.

2. *Why do you think Diana Baumrind feels that teaching by example is useful?*

Baumrind obviously feels that children are greatly influenced by the behavior of adults in their lives. She would probably say that "Do as I say, not as I do" is not an effective approach with young people, who tend to learn their behavior, like their language, by imitating the adults in their lives.

Can you think of any adults whose example influenced you—either positively or negatively? How has a particular example influenced who you are today?

3. *Baumrind encourages parents to show interest in children. What are some ways in which parents can show interest in children?*

In considering this answer, students can think about how adults showed—or did not show—interest in them as they grew up. Following are a few of the numerous possible ways adults can show interest in children:

- Reading out loud to children and asking their opinions about what was read
- Discussing the events of the children's day at dinnertime
- Asking children for their opinion on various matters, such as what color their room should be painted, what they think of their teachers, and so on.

4. *The authors feel that children are born with "their own inborn temperaments." Has your experience with children confirmed or contradicted their idea that children have different temperaments from the time they are born? Give some examples.*

Students can draw upon their experiences as siblings and/or parents. How alike or different were they from their siblings? How alike or different were their own children, or the children of someone close to them, from birth on?

4 ROWING THE BUS, Paul Logan

1. *Paul Logan titled his selection "Rowing the Bus." Yet very little of the essay actually deals with the incident the title describes—only the first and last paragraphs. Why do you think Logan chose that title?*

   Through his choice of title and by beginning with the rowing story and ending with a reference to it ("No one should have to row the bus"), Logan uses the image of rowing the bus to represent the cruelty and humiliation typical of situations involving bullies.

2. *Logan wanted to be kind to George, but he wanted even more to be accepted by the other students. Have you ever found yourself in a similar situation—where you wanted to do the right thing but felt that it had too high a price? Explain what happened.*

   Since bullies are everywhere, students are likely to have had experiences similar to Logan's. Thinking of bullies whom students have known may help jog their memories of relevant incidents.

3. *Logan refers to "a sinister code of childhood that demands there must always be someone to pick on." Why do children need someone to pick on?*

   Picking on someone allows a bully to feel stronger and better than that person—in his own eyes as well as in others'. This fact suggests that at least some bullies have fundamentally weak self-images.

4. *The novelist Henry James once said, "Three things in human life are important. The first is to be kind. The second is to be kind. And the third is to be kind." What do you think schools or concerned adults could do to encourage young people to treat one another with kindness, rather than with cruelty?*

   In addition to acting kindly themselves, teachers can use reading materials and school incidents to initiate discussions and raise students' consciousness about kindness.

   More specifically, what ways can you suggest to at least encourage young people not to bully? (Here are some things the schools can do to handle bullying: Use students and community volunteers to monitor playgrounds and lunchrooms and to help victims; provide martial-arts training to teach respect for others and self-confidence; institute a school policy making bullying an unacceptable offense.)

5   STUDENTS IN SHOCK, John Kellmayer

1. *If you were a peer counselor for Lisa or Dan, what advice might you give her or him?*

Lisa's desperation suggests that she must first address her emotional problems, perhaps even leaving school temporarily to gain emotional strength. Once she has dealt with her depression, she can seek rational ways to handle her financial problems and to settle on a major. Good college counselors can help her with both problems.

Dan would probably benefit greatly by doing just what he had thought of doing ("talking to somebody in the psychological counseling center," 5). If he had, he'd soon have realized that nothing is more "wrong with him" than with many other people struggling with a difficult situation. Like Lisa, Dan could also benefit from the guidance of a good vocational counselor.

2. *What were—or are—the most stressful parts of college life for you? Explain why. What ways have you found for dealing with that stress?*

Answers will vary, but many of the students' stresses undoubtedly will generally resemble those mentioned in the reading. Aspects of college life to consider include forming and maintaining personal support systems, dealing with financial pressure, choosing a major, learning study skills, and keeping up with class work.

3. *Kellmayer writes that "colleges . . . are trying in a number of ways to help students cope with the pressures they face." What resources does your college offer? Have you tried any? How do you think your school could improve the services it offers to help students deal with "student shock"?*

It may be helpful for the instructor to bring in materials explaining the counseling services available at the college and/or for a representative of the counseling services to come to class to explain what services are available and to answer questions. Students who have used some of the services at the college may wish to tell about their experiences, including whether or not they benefited and if so, how.

4. *On the basis of your college experience so far, what one piece of advice would you give to an incoming freshman?*

Students can draw upon their answers to question 2 in answering this question.

1. *Why do you suppose the incident in which Miss Bean threw an eraser at the author was such an "ice breaker"?*

    The incident was dramatic and funny and thus broke through the previous patterns of thought and behavior.

    Can you think of a dramatic and/or funny incident that occurred in any of your classes? What was it, and what change, if any, did it make in how people regarded someone?

2. *Have you ever experienced being in a school or class in which you were the only one of a certain group—the only student who was African American, white, Hispanic, older / younger, or different in some other way? What was it like? Did things get better or worse? Why?*

    Answers will vary. Students might also discuss similar situations at a place of work or in a neighborhood.

3. *Did you have any teachers that required you to think on your own? How did they get you to do so?*

    One way students might come up with answers to this question is by thinking of teachers from whom they gained confidence in their own ability to think. Did the teacher ask students for their opinions and judgments? Did he or she encourage differences of opinion in class?

4. *"Deadeye" Bean is Wilkins's favorite teacher. Who was your favorite high-school teacher, and why? Give an example of something special that teacher did, either for you or for the class.*

    Answers will vary. To get the discussion going, instructors may wish to give their own answers to this question.

7 NEW RESPECT FOR THE NAP, A PAUSE THAT REFRESHES, Jane E. Brody

1. *Are you a "napping enthusiast"? If so, when and where do you generally nap? How does napping affect you? After reading this article, do you agree that napping should, as Dr. Maas suggests, "have the status of daily exercise"?*

Answers will vary.

2. *According to Brody, companies recognize "that most of their employees are chronically sleep-deprived." Why do you think so many people get inadequate sleep? Do you or does anybody you know fail to get enough sleep? If so, how does it affect you or the other person?*

Here are a few common reasons that people are sleep deprived: They stay up late to watch favorite TV shows or participate in social events. They wake up frequently to care for babies. They have long commutes that add hours to their workday. After coming home from work, they are responsible for children/housework/elderly parents. They moonlight at a second job. They suffer from insomnia.
   Answers to the second and third parts of the question will vary.

3. *Brody argues that employers should promote napping at the workplace. How do you feel about such a proposal? What objections do you think employers might have to such a suggestion?*

Answers to the first part of the question will vary. Employers might object to the suggestion on the grounds that employees should be sleeping on their own time, not on company time. They might believe that rather than improving employee performance, allowing napping on the job will just make employees lazy.

4. *The NASA scientist's research showed that napping can improve a pilot's alertness and performance. What else (besides napping) do you think people could do to boost their alertness and performance, either in school or in the workplace?*

Some possible answers would include getting adequate sleep at night; getting exercise and fresh air during the workday (or schoolday); changing tasks frequently; or eating small nutritious snacks during the day.

8 GENDER INEQUALITY IN HEALTH CARE AND IN THE WORKPLACE, James M. Henslin

1. *Medical researchers discovered that men and women receive different health care because of "unintended sexual discrimination." How might such clear-cut discrimination be "unintended"? Do you know of any cases of gender health discrimination? Tell what happened.*

Discrimination might be unintended if the medical professionals involved do not recognize what they are doing. If they are in the habit of thinking that women exaggerate their symptoms or "go running to the doctor for every little thing," they may not take a woman's complaint as seriously as they would a man's. They may not intend to harm the woman, but their action still leads to a harmful outcome. Answers to the rest of the question will vary.

2. *According to Henslin, women suffer and men benefit from gender discrimination in the U.S. work force. Have you ever experienced or witnessed gender discrimination at work? Tell what happened.*

Answers will vary.

3. *Henslin states that a "quiet revolution" has taken place over the past century. Tell what you think are some of the changes he refers to when mentioning "a transformation in consumer patterns, relations at work, self-concepts, and relationships with boyfriends, husbands, and children." Also, describe any benefits or problems you feel may have been caused by the changes.*

Answers will vary, but students may mention such things as women having more say in important family purchases; women working in supervisory positions; men staying home to care for children; women earning more than their male partners; young girls seeing women role models in a variety of professional positions, etc.

4. *Did it surprise you to learn that in modern U.S. society, women earn significantly less than men? Explain. In your opinion, what are the causes of the gender gap, and what do you think would have to happen for it to end??*

Answers will vary.

1. *In her first meeting with the principal, Marta could have challenged him by telling what she had overheard the two teachers saying. Why do you think she stayed silent? What do you think the principal would have said or done if she'd told him she knew the real reason she wasn't being given the jacket?*

There could be several reasons why Marta didn't tell the principal what she had heard. She may have been afraid of seeming disrespectful to the principal. She may have been afraid of angering him or the teachers. She may have felt a misplaced sense of shame over what she had heard. She may have felt it was taboo to talk to the principal about racism.

The principal would surely have been worried and embarrassed if he knew what Marta had overheard. He might have denied it, claiming that Marta had misunderstood. He might have taken his anger out on her, accusing her of eavesdropping. Or he might have been so ashamed that he agreed to give her the jacket.

2. *Why do you think the principal gave in during his second meeting with Marta? What do you think that shows about Marta's grandfather's decision? What do you think might happen when the principal has to face the Board again? If you were the principal, what would you have said to the Board?*

The principal apparently recognized the truth of what Marta said—that if the jacket were paid for, it wouldn't be a scholarship jacket. He knew in his heart that Marta deserved the jacket. Clearly, Marta's grandfather made the right decision.

The principal will be in trouble with the Board. The members of the Board, which include Joann's father, apparently are more concerned with keeping the "important" people in the community happy than they are in recognizing true scholarship. The Board might even threaten the principal's job.

Answers to the third question will vary, but it seems likely that the principal will tell the Board that as an educator, he has to see the scholarship jacket given to the student who has earned it.

3. *Marta implies that she was discriminated against because of her racial background (she was Mexican) and her family's economic condition (they were poor). Have you ever experienced discrimination, or do you know of a friend who has experienced it? Explain.*

Answers will vary.

4. *Marta stresses again and again how important the scholarship jacket was to her and how hard she worked to win it. Is there something you worked hard to achieve when you were younger? How long did you work toward that goal? How did you feel when you finally succeeded—or did not succeed? What lessons, if any, did you learn from the experience?*

Answers will vary.

1. *Do you know anyone who has failed or almost failed a course? What effect did the experience have on that person?*

Answers will vary.

2. *Most people think of failing a course as a negative experience. Why, then, does Sherry consider the threat of failure to be a positive teaching tool? Do you agree?*

Sherry states that "the threat of flunking . . . is an expression of confidence by both teachers and parents that the students have the ability to learn the material presented to them" (11). This contrasts with the common practice of passing students who haven't mastered the basic skills, a practice that is excused "by saying kids can't learn if they come from terrible environments" (8). Sherry obviously believes most students can learn and that passing them without their having learned basic skills "dooms them to long-term illiteracy" (11).

3. *Besides the threat of failure, what are some other ways that teachers can motivate students? What have teachers done to make you want to work harder for a class?*

Answers will vary. As Sherry implies in paragraph 4, a teacher's style is one important factor in gaining students' attention and getting them to work harder. The more interested a student is in a class, the harder he or she will probably work. Other ideas teachers have used include providing rewards for good work, such as praise and awards; bringing people with interesting careers into class to inform and motivate students; and using reading materials that are relevant to students' lives.

4. *People often look back on their education and realize that some of the teachers they learned the most from were their strictest teachers. Who do you think you learned most from, strict teachers or lenient ones? Give examples to support your point.*

Answers will vary. A discussion on this question might benefit from first describing just what a strict teacher is. Some characteristics of strict teachers are providing challenging work, expecting students to do all assignments on time, and handing out good grades only for good work.

SUGGESTED ANSWERS TO THE DISCUSSION QUESTIONS IN PART II

Note: The numbers in parentheses refer to paragraphs in the reading. For some questions, additional related questions have been included to enhance class discussion.

1 THE YELLOW RIBBON, Pete Hamill

1. According to the information in the selection, what is Vingo's attitude toward his wife?

Vingo clearly loves his wife and hopes that she will take him back, although he has left the decision up to her and expects the worst (17–19). While in prison, he wrote to her, "I understand if you can't stay married to me." He even suggested the possibility that she'd find "a new guy— she's a wonderful woman, really something" (17). He has told her not to write to him and has even spared her the possible pain of seeing him again: if she doesn't want him back, all she has to do is *not* tie the yellow handkerchief to the tree (19). He shows "a cracked, much-handled snapshot" of his wife and family to the young people (21)—further evidence of his love.

What might his wife's feelings have been upon learning her husband had to go to prison? Why might she not have written to him for three and a half years?

2. Has Vingo assumed responsibility for his crime, in your opinion?

Answers will vary, but they should take into consideration the fact that Vingo said, "I did it and I went to jail. If you can't do the time, don't do the crime" (13).

3. While there is much we don't learn about Vingo in this very short narrative, Hamill does provide us with clues to some important aspects of his personality. What evidence is there that he is a decent man, a person who we could feel deserves a second chance?

- Vingo's "cocoon of silence" (2) suggests that he sometimes dealt with important issues very introspectively. He does not seem afraid of coming to terms with his feelings.

- He is willing to take responsibility for himself and others. He took responsibility for his actions by accepting the idea that he earned imprisonment: "I did it and I went to jail. If you can't do the time, don't do the crime" (13). This also suggests that Vingo took some responsibility in making a point of showing young people the hazards of crime.

- He was probably ashamed of what he did and did not expect his wife to be loyal to him any more (17–19). This shows, again, his understanding of his errors and willingness to own up to them.

- When it came to his family, he was appreciative and loving (17–21). He is also unselfish in freeing his wife from any responsibility towards him while he is in prison and even suggesting she find "a new guy" (17). His words to her reveal that he places her feelings and needs ahead of his.

- He has a personality that attracted the young people to him and made them—and his wife!— care about him (21).

4. *Many people are thrilled, some even to tears, by this story. What makes "The Yellow Ribbon" have such a powerful effect on readers?*

Like the young people, the reader begins to care a lot about Vingo and his fate. He is at a turning point in his life, and what happens at the tree means a great deal in terms of both his past and his future. We all can empathize with anticipation of such moments. Hamill accents the drama of that moment by building up to it and saving it for last. This moment is especially meaningful because it represents that which we all seek—unconditional love. We all want to have someone ready to fill up a tree with ribbons of acceptance of us and to take us back into his or her life, no matter what mistakes we have made. We all want forgiveness and the right to a second chance.

2   URBAN LEGENDS, Beth Johnson

1. *Johnson writes that urban legends "teach us lessons." Which of the stories in the article do you think teaches the most effective lesson?*

Answers will vary, but perhaps the most effective lessons are taught by the most horrible legends—the ones in which the person who has broken the unwritten rule is punished most dreadfully. Therefore, the "lover's lane" and "spider in the hairdo" stories might be considered most effective.

2. *Have you ever heard any of the stories described, but in slightly different form? Or have you heard any story that is so dramatic that you wonder if it is true or not? Retell any such story you have heard, as best as you can remember it.*

A few other common urban legends that may come up are those about alligators in the sewers, a drug-crazed babysitter who put a baby in the microwave, poisonous serpents or spiders hidden in imported goods, persons being charged large sums for a recipe (often for cake) they'd requested from a restaurant, and a dead teenager who reappears to strangers on the anniversary of her death.
   Where did you first hear this story? What about it made it believable?

3. *Johnson claims that "we haven't quite given up our need for scary stories that are a little too good to be true." In our culture, where else besides urban legends do we find such stories?*

Scary movies, such as the *Friday the 13th* and *Halloween* series, and horror stories, such as those by Stephen King, are extremely popular sources of chills similar to those in urban legends.

4. *Frightening stories, whether in movies or in novels such as those by Stephen King, are a large part of our entertainment. In your opinion, why might people so enjoy being scared?*

Fright, like any other strong emotion, is stimulating. Perhaps we enjoy frightening stories because they provide a "safe" source of that stimulus—we're scared, but also aware that we're not actually in danger. We may enjoy sharing a frightening experience, such as at the movies or while exchanging urban legends, because the accompanying shrieking and excitement provide an outlet for tension we are feeling.
   What are some other frightening experiences that we deliberately seek out?

3   SHAME, Dick Gregory

1. *Why did Gregory include both the classroom and the restaurant anecdotes in one selection? What is the difference between the shame he felt in the first incident and the shame he felt in the second? What are the similarities between the two incidents?*

Had "Shame" not included the anecdote abut the wino, it would have focused on only one type of shame, that shame people feel when others look down on them (5, 6), ignore their feelings (16–22), and feel sorry for them (28, sentence 2). The story about the wino introduces another type of shame. This type of shame—which Gregory felt when he "waited too long to help another man"—results when someone makes another person feel the first type of shame.

The similarity between the two incidents is that in both cases someone has not taken another unfortunate person's feelings into account. In the first anecdote, Gregory is on the receiving end of inconsiderate behavior. In the second, he is the inconsiderate one. He seems to be saying that the shame he felt in the second case was much greater.

2. *What could Gregory mean by the sentence "The eagle always flew on Friday" (paragraph 7)? What does this fact reveal about his world?*

"The eagle" is a reference to the eagle on the silver dollar and is used to symbolize people's paychecks, received on Friday. The statement that the eagle "flew" implies people spent their paychecks quickly. This in turn implies a working-class society in which people live from paycheck to paycheck.

3. *One type of irony is an event or an effect that is the opposite of what might be expected. In what ways are the following parts of "Shame" ironic?*

   • *I never learned hate at home, or shame. I had to go to school for that.*

   The irony here is that school is meant to teach us something better than shame.

   • *If I knew my place and didn't come too close, she'd wink at me and say hello. That was a good feeling.*

   We might not expect someone to feel good about knowing his "place" and keeping his distance.

   • *I looked at the wino with blood all over his face and I went over. "Leave him alone, Mister Williams. I'll pay the twenty-six cents."*
   The wino got up . . . . He looked at me with pure hate.

   We would not expect a response that seems to be generous to be met with "pure hate."

   In each of these cases, Gregory makes us think twice about how people make each other feel. In so doing, he enriches our understanding of his descriptions of shame.

4. *Has anyone ever tried to help you in a way that didn't take all your needs into account? If so, how did you feel toward that person? In what ways might activities that are meant to help people also hurt them?*

Answers will vary. Possible avenues of discussion include ways our social agencies help people, how family members help and hurt each other, and how schools sometimes teach negative lessons instead of positive ones.

1. *Have you ever been in a situation where the bystander effect played a part? Would your behavior be any different in light of what you have learned from this article?*

Answers will vary.

2. *The author states in paragraph 31, "Bystanders look to others for cues as to what is happening. Frequently other witnesses, just as confused, try to look calm." Why do you think witnesses would try to look calm during an emergency?*

Answers will vary. A possible clue is in paragraph 29: "Bystanders are afraid to endanger themselves or look foolish if they take the wrong action in a situation they're not sure how to interpret." Rather than reveal their fear or confusion, they might mask it with pretense: I'm in control; I know what's really going on; this isn't as bad as it looks (and therefore doesn't warrant my interference).

3. *In paragraph 33, the author suggests that if you understand what causes "the bystander effect," you can act appropriately in an emergency: "If you take action, others may also help." If, say, you were in a group of onlookers while a fight was in progress, what could you do that would encourage others to intervene?*

The article implies that whatever you do to weaken the level of ambiguity will encourage bystander intervention (29). Thus any action that can be readily interpreted by others to mean they are not in danger and will not look foolish would be encouraging. Perhaps such actions will also remind bystanders that group morality (32) tends to be influenced by individual actions.

4. *How does the conclusion of this article clarify the author's purpose for the reader? How does the article's beginning fit in with that purpose?*

Paragraphs 2–32 present only the facts about the bystander effect. Thus without its beginning and conclusion, the article would appear to be written simply to inform the reader. By raising the issue of the reader's "appropriate action" (33), however, the ending reveals the author's persuasive purpose—to convince readers to overcome the bystander effect. The beginning of the article also points to that purpose by raising the question of how readers, rather than hypothetical people, would respond in certain emergency situations.

5 THE REAL STORY OF FLIGHT 93, Karen Breslau, Eleanor Clift, and Evan Thomas

1. *Where were you on the terrible day of September 11th, 2001, and what were your reactions to the events of that day?*

   Answers will vary.

2. *How did reading this selection affect you? For example, as you were reading, did you feel pity, anger, horror, surprise, admiration, pride, or a combination of the above? Explain.*

   Answers will vary, but most students will react to the selection with a combination of emotions.

3. *While the selection focuses mainly on the struggle between a group of passengers and the hijackers, we are also given specific details about individual passengers. Which details would you say are particularly effective in making you see these people as individuals? If you could interview any of the passengers, whom would you choose, and what questions would you want to ask?*

   Students will probably mention the personal details about individual passengers in paragraph 17, revealing these passengers' physical strength and ability to cope with crisis or danger, and the quoted excerpts from telephone calls, which attest to the passengers' courage and selflessness. Answers to the second question will vary.

4. *The authors of this selection—and people throughout the world—have celebrated the passengers of Flight 93 as true heroes. Do you agree with this view? Why or why not? In stating your case, compare your personal definition of the word* hero *with the behaviors of the passengers.*

   Answers will vary.

6 COPING WITH NERVOUSNESS, Rudolph F. Verderber

1. *What have your public speaking experiences been like? Have some speeches gone better than others? If so, what were the differences, and what do you think were the reasons for those differences? What did you find helpful in preparing and giving speeches?*

Answers will vary.

2. *Why might it be a good idea to speak on a topic you know a great deal about and are interested in? Can you think of any examples from the speeches you've given or heard?*

Verderber writes, "If you feel in command of your material . . . , you'll be far more confident" (9). A speaker will certainly be in command of material when the topic is one that he or she knows a great deal about. With such a topic, a speaker isn't just memorizing facts and ideas; he or she is putting into words ideas that are very familiar.

3. *You may need to give speeches in your classes, but do you think you will have to speak in public after you graduate from school? In what situations might you have to give a speech or even a presentation to a small group?*

People in such fields as politics and religion may routinely have to give speeches, but people in a variety of other arenas also must speak before groups. Following are some examples:

- A company manager presents new information to the ten people in his or her department
- A Sunday school instructor teaches a lesson to thirty students
- A volunteer gives a report at a meeting attended by fifty others
- A firefighter explains safety rules to an auditorium full of students
- A salesperson reports on his or her department at a company meeting

4. *Obviously, Verderber feels that nervousness is no reason to avoid speaking in public. What other activities have you willingly done despite the fact that they made you nervous in some way? Was being nervous in these situations helpful in some ways? If so, how?*

Answers will vary. Following are some other activities that people do for various reasons despite the fact that they make them nervous:

- Asking someone out on a date
- Going for a job interview
- Taking the writing and driving tests for a driver's license
- Getting married in front of a crowd of family and friends

7 COMPLIANCE TECHNIQUES, Shelley E. Taylor, Letitia Anne Peplau, and David O. Sears

1. *While reading this selection, did you recognize techniques that have been used to influence you to make a purchase or support someone's plan? How were the techniques used?*

   Answers will vary. Situations in which such techniques are commonly used include calls from charitable organizations, sales calls, sales ads, bargaining, and in-store pricing.

2. *Which of the compliance techniques do you feel is most clearly deceptive? Why?*

   Answers will vary, but the only technique pointed out by the authors as being clearly deceptive is the low-ball technique, about which they write

   > Essentially, the person is tricked into agreeing to a relatively attractive proposition, only to discover later that the terms are actually different from those expected. . . . Although this technique can be effective . . . , it is clearly deceptive . . . laws have been enacted to make low-balling illegal for several industries. (11)

3. *The authors state that no one is really sure why the "foot in the door" technique is effective, but they offer two possible explanations. Does either of those explanations seem to you to adequately explain why the technique works? Can you think of an alternative explanation?*

   Answers will vary. A possible third explanation may be that people feel refusing the second request will appear to be backing off from their original commitment, something they are embarrassed to do.

4. *Imagine that you are in the business of selling home computers. Describe how you would use the foot-in-the-door technique, the door-in-the-face technique, and the low-ball technique to try to make a sale.*

   A *foot-in-the-door technique* to sell home computers might be to ask customers to rent a computer for a short time. Once a customer views himself or herself as a computer user, he or she might be more willing to buy. A *door-in-the-face technique* to sell home computers might involve asking a customer to buy the top-of-the-line computer and then offering something notably less expensive. In a *low-ball technique* to sell home computers, the customer might at first be told only the price of the computer itself. Once the customer shows interest, then the salesperson would add on the prices of necessary adjuncts to the computer—the software and the printer.

8   LIZZIE BORDEN, James Kirby Martin and others

1. *Based on the information in the reading, do you agree or disagree with the experts who say Lizzie was guilty? Explain your answer.*

Answers will vary.

2. *As you read this selection, what impression did you form of life in the Borden household? What particular details helped you form that opinion?*

In paragraph 2, the authors provide various details to show how for Lizzie (and Emma) "life in the flats was an intolerable embarrassment" and grim. Furthermore, the authors show that Lizzie's parents themselves added to the discomfort of the household: In paragraphs 1 and 2, Andrew is depicted as ungenerous and unamusing, and in paragraph 2 we are told that Lizzie "strongly disliked" her stepmother.

3. *The authors imply that the story about Andrew Borden's cutting off the feet of corpses to make them fit undersized coffins was a rumor, not a proved fact. Why, then, do you think they include the story in this piece?*

The story is a colorful, dramatic example of Borden's reputation. Even if the story isn't true, the details of the selection suggest that the character implications behind the story are true.

4. *Do you believe that any of the notions about women that existed in Lizzie Borden's day are still at work in some ways today? Explain your answer.*

Following are the notions about women mentioned in the selection:

- "Society expected a woman of social position to marry, and while she waited for a proper suitor, her only respectable social outlets were church and community service" (3).
- "A woman of Lizzie's social position, they affirmed, simply could not have committed such a terrible crime" (7).
- "'Americans were certain that well-brought up daughters could not commit murder with a hatchet on sunny summer mornings.' Criminal women, they believed, originated in the lower classes and even looked evil" (8).
- "Jurors and editorialists alike judged Lizzie according to their preconceived notions of Victorian womanhood. They believed that such a woman was gentle, docile, and physically frail, short on analytical ability but long on nurturing instincts" (9).
- "'Women,' wrote an editorialist for Scribner's, 'are merely large babies. They are shortsighted, frivolous, and occupy an intermediate stage between children and men'" (9).
- "Too uncoordinated and weak to accurately swing an ax and too gentle and unintelligent to coldly plan a double murder, women of Lizzie's background simply had to be innocent because of their basic innocence" (9).

To what extent are any of the above points of view still at work today? What examples of women are there in American society today—and in other countries—that contradict the above views?

9 NONVERBAL COMMUNICATION, Anthony F. Grasha

1. *What are your answers to the following questions from the selection? Why do you think the author included these questions?*

    *   *Why do you think we allow a doctor to easily violate our intimate distance zone?*

        We give the goal of maintaining and improving our health priority over other considerations. The question, however, is a reminder that despite that goal, many of us are still uncomfortable when the doctor does "violate our intimate distance zone." Like the following two questions, this question underlines the intensity of our feelings about those zones.

    *   *I can remember becoming angry and generally irritated when a friend of mine placed a plate and glass in my space. . . . Has this ever happened to you?*

        Students may think of similar situations, such as someone sitting closer to them than the distance other people were sitting from each other at a table.

    *   *What would violate the social distance norms in a classroom?*

        Such violations might include a girl sitting on her boyfriend's lap, the teacher discussing his or her personal problems in class, and somebody knitting during a lecture.

2. *This selection includes headings, italics, labels, and numbered items. How are these related to the author's purpose?*

    The author's purpose is to inform. By helping readers to be aware of the article's enumerations and organization, he is helping them to understand and remember the information he presents.
      How does this structure relate to the benefits of outlining a reading?

3. *What are some examples of a dating or business situation in which someone's body language might contradict his or her verbal communication?*

    Grasha explains that "we have less conscious control over the specific body gestures or expressions we might make while talking." Thus whenever we say one thing and mean another, our body language is likely to contradict what we say. There are therefore many possible answers to this question, including the following:

    *   In a conversation with someone at a party, we might appear to be listening and responding, but our eyes may be looking around the room for a more interesting person to talk to.
    *   During a job evaluation, we might be saying "yes" to our supervisor's suggestions for changes, but our arms might be crossed and our jaw clenched, indicating we do not agree with his or her recommendations.

      What other postures, facial expressions, hand and arm movements might give away the fact that a person is saying one thing but means another?

4. *Give examples from your own experience of all four types of personal space.*

    Answers will vary.

1. If you had lived in preindustrial days, do you think you would have chosen to live in a city or in a rural area? Why?

People choosing to live in the city may cite the possibility of developing a profession that would not be possible in the country, the excitement of having new people constantly around, or cultural or entertainment possibilities. Country-dwellers might prefer the quieter, more routine life of the small village, the relative cleanliness of the country, and the more close-knit life of a small group of people living near one another.

Does thinking about this choice clarify some of your priorities in life?

2. What draws people to or keeps them in big cities today? Compare these reasons with those which attracted newcomers to preindustrial cities.

People in some professions today feel they can only really "make it" in a large city, where they have plenty of opportunities to practice their skills. They are drawn by the arts and entertainment possibilities there, the cultural mix of the population, or the feeling of being at the center of the action. People moving to preindustrial cities were probably drawn to them for similar reasons. Although there would not have been the kind of international mix of population there is in cities today, travelers coming from different areas of England, for example, may have been almost equally exotic to one another. The rapid spread of information today makes it less likely that people can leave their old identities behind when they move to the city.

3. The radius of preindustrial cities was "usually no more than three miles from the center." What factors have allowed today's huge cities and their suburbs to exist?

Today's cities and suburbs can sprawl over miles because of the development of modern highways and transportation; the ease with which information can be moved from one end of the city to another via newspapers, television, and radio; the development of the computer, which makes it possible for people working in different locations to share information; and the development of institutions (schools, hospitals, etc.) that serve all areas within the cities.

4. According to the reading, preindustrial city dwellers had to protect themselves from the filth and crime in big cities. How are problems of city dwellers today the same or different?

Preindustrial cities were filthy throughout, but today's cities tend to be dirtiest in the poorer sections, leading the residents there to feel bitter towards city government. Although violence and crime existed in the preindustrial cities, drug use and feelings of alienation in today's cities may lead to more acts of random violence. Disease spread quickly through preindustrial cities because of crowding and poor hygiene. Today, the health-care system in large cities is often overworked, especially with regard to treating the poor, so disease prevention and care are often inadequate.

TEST BANKS

This section contains the following:

- A **First Test Bank** (pages 43–130) consisting of four additional Mastery Tests for each chapter in Part One of *Ten Steps to Improving College Reading Skills*, Fourth Edition, as well as four additional Combined-Skills Mastery Tests;
- A **Second Test Bank** (pages 135–182) consisting of copies of the tests on the computer software that is available with the book.

> *NOTE:* **Instructors who have assigned the software tests should not also use this Second Test Bank,** as it duplicates the material in the software. The software tests are printed here as a convenience for these instructors and also as a supplementary test bank for instructors who are **not** using the software with students.

Instructors whose students are using *Ten Steps to Improving College Reading Skills*, Fourth Edition, in class have permission to reproduce any of these tests on a photocopying machine as often as needed.

The answer key for the First Test Bank is on pages 131–134; for the Second Test Bank, on pages 183–184.

VOCABULARY IN CONTEXT: Test A

A. For each item below, underline the **examples** that suggest the meaning of the italicized term. Then, in the space provided, write the letter of the meaning of that term.

___ 1. Most daydreams concern such *mundane* events as paying the telephone bill and picking up the groceries.
    A. complicated   C. proper
    B. ordinary   D. exciting

___ 2. Everyone has their *foibles,* and I admit that mine include eating with my hands and being late everywhere I go.
    A. strengths   C. hobbies
    B. minor faults   D. crimes

___ 3. The supervisor's day was filled with one minor *calamity* after another. In the morning, his car broke down; at lunchtime, he lost his wallet; and at the end of the day, his computer crashed and he lost a day's work.
    A. requirement   C. question
    B. claim   D. disaster

B. Each item below includes a word or words that are a **synonym** of the italicized word. Write the synonym of the italicized word in the space provided.

_____ 4. You can't do algebra until you have mastered *rudimentary* math skills—basic addition, subtraction, multiplication, and division.

_____ 5. Love is not always considered a *prerequisite* for marriage. In some cultures, social status or economic potential is a more important requirement.

_____ 6. According to recent studies, a shortage of sleep due to long work or study hours will not cause any permanent damage to your health. One good night of sleep, researchers say, can make up for a week of sleep *deficit.*

C. Each item below includes a word or words that are an **antonym** of the italicized word. Underline the antonym of each italicized word. Then write the letter of the meaning of the italicized word.

___ 7. The children wanted us to adopt an older German shepherd from the pound, but we were told he was rather wild, so instead we chose a collie that was more *docile.*
    A. manageable   C. expensive
    B. disobedient   D. temporary   *(Continues on next page)*

___ 8. Though the United States is one of the most *affluent* nations in the world, one in four children grow up in poor circumstances.
   A. famous
   B. active
   C. wealthy
   D. large

D. Use the **general sense of each sentence** to figure out the meaning of each italicized word. Then write the letter of the meaning of the italicized word.

___ 9. The journalism instructor *denounced* local news shows for emphasizing crime, fires, and the like at the expense of more important city issues.
   A. stopped
   B. joined
   C. admired
   D. criticized

___10. After a hundred years of its "boys only" policy, a military school finally decided to *deviate* from its tradition and let females in.
   A. depart
   B. borrow
   C. learn
   D. accept

VOCABULARY IN CONTEXT: Test B

A. For each item below, underline the **examples** that suggest the meaning of the italicized term. Then, in the space provided, write the letter of the meaning of that term.

___ 1. I'm happy sightseeing *vicariously*, for instance, through travel TV shows and magazines.
   A. personally   C. indirectly
   B. expensively   D. energetically

___ 2. There are good reasons to think TV has a *detrimental* influence on kids. After all, TV watching keeps them from exercising, encourages them to eat unhealthy foods, and teaches them to be violent.
   A. deadly   C. strong
   B. dull   D. harmful

B. Each item below includes a word or words that are a **synonym** of the italicized word. Write the synonym of the italicized word in the space provided.

_____ 3. New inventions make old ones *obsolete*. For instance, because of the compact disk, the phonograph record is now outdated.

_____ 4. During the fourteenth century, the Black Death *decimated* one third of the population of Europe. Two centuries later, smallpox wiped out 95 percent of the native population of Mexico.

_____ 5. Until recently, immunization seemed to have erased the *peril* of diseases such as measles, rubella, and mumps, but now the threat of these dangerous illnesses is growing.

C. Each item below includes a word or words that are an **antonym** of the italicized word. Underline the antonym of each italicized word. Then write the letter of the meaning of the italicized word.

___ 6. To a person at a peaceful lakeshore, the environment seems silent. But to the sensitive ears of a dog, the same lake may be a *clamorous* place filled with the buzzing of insects and the bustling of small animals.
   A. natural   C. boring
   B. noisy   D. dangerous

(Continues on next page)

___ 7. Some scientists think dreams express hidden wishes and desires. Others disagree, arguing instead that dreams deal with more *overt* concerns, such as the people and problems in our everyday lives.

    A. obvious   C. damaging

    B. informal   D. mysterious

___ 8. While the passion of love may *wane* over time, intimacy tends to grow. This change often results in a more rewarding connection than the emotional roller coaster that is often the case in the early stages of relationships.

    A. frighten   C. lessen

    B. expand   D. transfer

D. Use the **general sense of each sentence** to figure out the meaning of each italicized word. Then write the letter of the meaning of the italicized word.

___ 9. Watching television is, above all, a *passive* experience. One sits back and waits to be entertained.

    A. complicated   C. aggressive

    B. expensive   D. inactive

___10. Today many young couples are *ambivalent* about having children; they cannot decide which is more important—pursuing their careers or building a family.

    A. knowledgeable   C. sure

    B. having mixed feelings   D. tired

VOCABULARY IN CONTEXT: Test C

Using context clues for help, write the letter of the best meaning for each italicized word or words.

___ 1. Grasshoppers are a prized food in some places, but most people in Western societies find them *repugnant.*
- A. delightful
- B. disgusting
- C. confusing
- D. filling

___ 2. My brother's irresponsible work habits are gradually *eroding* his boss's confidence in him.
- A. equal to
- B. building
- C. wearing away
- D. preserving

___ 3. I want to teach my children to be *wary* of strangers without making them overly fearful of people they don't know.
- A. neighborly
- B. careful
- C. unsuspecting
- D. surprised

___ 4. Even while in the womb, a baby can *discriminate* between the voice of its mother and that of another woman.
- A. be confused
- B. cry
- C. distinguish
- D. play

___ 5. After winning the basketball championship, the players *flaunted* their victory by screaming over and over, "We won."
- A. lied about
- B. exaggerated
- C. forgot
- D. showed off

___ 6. People who experience too much stress are *prone* to such health problems as flu, sore throat, headaches, and backaches.
- A. likely to have
- B. protected
- C. responding
- D. too busy for

___ 7. The time we spend dreaming *dwindles* over our lifetimes. Babies dream as much as eight hours a day, but adults dream less than two hours each night.
- A. passes
- B. shrinks
- C. connects
- D. adds up

___ 8. A generation or two ago, it was considered rude to bring up three topics in polite conversation—politics, religion, and sex, but nowadays we do not *adhere to* such limitations.
- A. change
- B. mind
- C. follow
- D. question

(Continues on next page)

___ 9. When speaking to a large audience, it is helpful to remember that people are *egocentric*. They pay closest attention to messages about their own values, their own beliefs, and their own well-being.
   A. self-centered
   B. impatient
   C. understanding
   D. self-controlled

___10. The chapter ended with the hero in the *precarious* position of hanging from a cliff.
   A. unimportant
   B. ordinary
   C. cautious
   D. dangerous

VOCABULARY IN CONTEXT: Test D

Using context clues for help, write the letter of the best meaning for each italicized word or words.

___ 1. Open communication can lead to healthier relationships. Research shows that couples who often *disclose* their feelings to each other report having stronger feelings of love and happiness than others.
   A. change   C. reveal
   B. forget   D. foresee

___ 2. In a political cartoon, the senator was *depicted* as a baseball player who struck out.
   A. photographed   C. joined
   B. represented   D. quoted

___ 3. There is still a great *discrepancy* between the wages the sexes earn. For every dollar that men make, women earn only seventy-two cents.
   A. similarity   C. advantage
   B. logic   D. difference

___ 4. In addition to working full-time at the bank, Emilio *augments* his income during the holiday season by working several nights a week at a local department store.
   A. replaces   C. overlooks
   B. saves   D. adds to

___ 5. In intense summer heat and humidity, I feel so *lackadaisical* that all I want to do is sleep, eat, and then sleep some more.
   A. angry   C. lazy
   B. well-off   D. ill

___ 6. The manager said not only is it *feasible* to repair the tire instead of replacing it, but it is also possible to have it done by tonight.
   A. achievable   C. late
   B. unreasonable   D. early

___ 7. In the 1950s, the nation's *flourishing* economy provided middle-class people with the money they needed to buy new homes outside of overcrowded urban areas. Thus the movement from the cities to the suburbs grew.
   A. failing   C. farm
   B. successful   D. dried-up

___ 8. Jimmy made several *overtures* to the new boy next door, including inviting him to a barbecue and asking him to play with his friends.
   A. invitations   C. excuses
   B. remarks   D. jokes

(Continues on next page)

_____ 9. Scientists find that when people feel "love at first sight," the pleasure center of the brain releases a chemical that *stimulates* the body, causing rapid heartbeat, giddiness, and deep breathing.

A. makes more active   C. bypasses

B. quiets down   D. imitates

_____10. In ancient Greece, love had been regarded as somewhat undesirable, a divine punishment. By the twelfth century, poets in Europe had taken this *notion* even further; love, they argued, was a sweet form of suffering.

A. reason   C. hope

B. punishment   D. idea

MAIN IDEAS: Test A

The following selections have topic sentences (main ideas) that may appear at any place within the paragraph. Identify the topic sentence of each paragraph by filling in the correct sentence number in the space provided.

____ 1. ¹Often when older children move back home, unpleasant tensions and disagreements arise. ²However, adult children who move back home can avoid family conflicts by following some tips. ³First, they should contribute what they can—and it need not be in terms of money: Being productive family members will help them earn their keep. ⁴This can involve tutoring or coaching younger sisters or brothers, or helping Mom and Dad with chores and errands. ⁵Second, these "returnees" should not expect their parents to rescue them from difficulties. ⁶As adults, they are responsible for getting out of their own scrapes—and for trying to avoid them in the first place. ⁷Last, they must respect their parents' lifestyles and own needs for independence. ⁸It is unrealistic to expect parents' lives to revolve around the needs of a grown child, in the manner they may have when the child was younger.

____ 2. ¹Scientists have learned that the way we view exercise strongly influences our performance. ²Research on Russian weight lifters, for example, demonstrated that if they were told the weights were heavy, they perceived an exercise to be more difficult. ³If they were told the weights were light, then they considered the exercise easier. ⁴Another example is the weight lifter who kept failing to break a record. ⁵He finally succeeded after his trainer told him the weights he was lifting were not as heavy as they in fact were.

____ 3. ¹Until the 1940s, most Americans were born and died at home. ²Births and deaths happened when they happened, often without medical intervention. ³If a baby was too premature or defective or if a seriously ill person was dying, there was little the family doctor could do about it other than to offer comfort. ⁴Today, most Americans are born and die in hospitals under the supervision of medical personnel who sometimes decide to keep them alive long beyond the point at which they would normally have died. ⁵Patients can be hooked up for days, months, or years to machines that sustain their lives. ⁶This step may be taken even if they are in constant pain or permanently comatose. ⁷Obviously, technology has greatly changed how we are born and die.

(Continues on next page)

___ 4. [1]Though natural-fiber purists may turn up their noses at it, polyester-and-cotton-blend clothing has advantages over all-cotton garments. [2]For one thing, polyester, which is manufactured, costs less than cotton, which grows naturally but is expensive to process. [3]Therefore, cotton/polyester clothing is more economical than pure cotton garments. [4]Also, the polyester content of cotton-blend clothing helps the garments retain their shape after repeated washings. [5]That's because this synthetic does not share cotton's tendency to shrink or stretch after immersion. [6]But perhaps polyester's most endearing quality is its "no-wrinkle policy." [7]Unlike pure cotton, polyester blends require little or no ironing!

___ 5. [1]Baseball enthusiasts hold softball in low esteem. [2]It's a picnic game, they argue, with a big, soft ball, shorter base paths, and a pitcher who throws underhand. [3]Yet fast-pitch softball can be as intense and dramatic as any baseball game, perhaps more so. [4]True, the base paths are shorter, but ask any third baseman how quickly a well-hit groundball reaches him on softball's smaller diamond. [5]True, the pitcher throws underhand, but he stands fifteen feet closer to the plate, and he might hit speeds exceeding eighty miles per hour. [6]True, the ball is softer than a baseball, but catch a hard one in the ribs just once, and such knowledge is small comfort.

MAIN IDEAS: Test B

The following selections have topic sentences (main ideas) that may appear at any place within the paragraph. Identify the topic sentence of each paragraph by filling in the correct sentence number in the space provided.

___ 1. [1]Plastic trash bags were once considered a major menace to the environment. [2]The makers of plastic trash bags responded to the environmental concerns and made several positive changes in their product. [3]First, they made use of a new additive—actually, potato peels—to make the bags biodegradable (that is, capable of breaking down and being absorbed by the environment). [4]Next, they removed any ingredients in their plastic formula which would contaminate soil in a landfill. [5]Finally, they made it possible for the bags to be burned safely, without adding dangerous pollutants to the air.

___ 2. [1]Snoring is the number-one complaint in marriages all around the world. [2]The honks, hoots, and snorts created by snorers annoy their mates and deprive them of sleep. [3]Fortunately, there are some means of preventing snoring. [4]First, the snorer should avoid breathing through his mouth. [5]Mouth-breathing can be discouraged if the snorer sleeps on his side with his forearm under his chin—effectively pressing his mouth shut. [6]Second, the snorer should increase the humidity in his bedroom. [7]A humidifier or even a pot of water in the room may help. [8]In addition, snoring may disappear if an overweight snorer loses some pounds. [9]And finally, a snorer should avoid drinking alcohol in the evening.

___ 3. [1]A young girl looks at a fashion magazine and sees clothes modeled by women carrying 115 pounds on their five-foot-ten-inch frames. [2]She receives a "teen doll" as a present and studies its proportions: legs nearly two-thirds the length of its body, tiny waist, non-existent hips and thighs. [3]She goes to the movies and observes screen heroines who in their leanness resemble adolescent boys more than mature women. [4]Her favorite television shows are filled with commercials for weight-loss programs that equate slenderness with desirability. [5]By the time the girl reaches her teens, she has been thoroughly bombarded with society's message that to be thin is the only acceptable option.

(Continues on next page)

___ 4. ¹Symbols can have a tremendously powerful emotional impact upon us, instantly conveying many feelings and ideas. ²Symbols like the cross, the Star of David, or the star-and-crescent immediately make us think of the Christian, Jewish, or Muslim religions. ³This may be why burning an American flag often arouses more anger than does an attack on the values for which the flag actually stands. ⁴Another symbol with terrible power is the swastika. ⁵Until this century, the swastika was an innocent traditional symbol found in many cultures. ⁶Then it became the symbol of Nazi terror. ⁷Today, the very sight of a swastika can send chills down our spines.

___ 5. ¹Can psychics see into the future? ²Although one might wish for a psychic stock forecaster, the tallied forecasts of "leading psychics" reveal little accuracy. ³In one eight-year period, the New Year's predictions of the *National Enquirer*'s favorite psychics yielded two accurate predictions out of 486. ⁴During the early 1990s, tabloid psychics were all wrong in predicting surprising events (Madonna did not become a gospel singer, a UFO base was not found in the Mexican desert, Queen Elizabeth did not abdicate her throne to enter a convent). ⁵And they missed all the significant unexpected events, such as the breakup of the Soviet Union, Saddam Hussein's assault on Kuwait, and the O.J. Simpson case. ⁶Before 1994, psychics offered many predictions about Michael Jackson—that he would marry Oprah Winfrey, become a traveling evangelist, and have a sex-change operation—but missed their chance to predict his marriage to Lisa Marie Presley.

MAIN IDEAS: Test C

The following textbook excerpts have topic sentences (main ideas) that may appear at any place within the paragraph. Identify the topic sentence of each paragraph by filling in the correct sentence number in the space provided.

___ 1. [1]For many years, there has been a section in *Reader's Digest* magazine called "Laughter, the Best Medicine." [2]The name is not such an exaggeration—medical studies show that laughter is good for one's physical and emotional health. [3]A hearty laugh exercises the internal organs, including the heart and lungs. [4]The deep breathing that accompanies laughter supplies your body with extra oxygen. [5]Many diseases deplete the body's supply of oxygen, so getting extra oxygen is important. [6]Laughter may also stimulate the body's production of endorphins, which act as painkillers and antidepressants.

___ 2. [1]Scientists predict that textbooks of the future will be computerized and will thus offer many of the special benefits unique to computers. [2]First of all, they say that the books will take the form of small plastic cards that can be inserted into screens the size of paperback novels. [3]Viewers will be able to select the size and style of print and automatic page turning, or they may choose to listen to an audio version and just watch the pictures. [4]They will be able to zoom in for close-ups of illustrations, which will then fill the screen and rotate for a three-dimensional view, so that medical students, for example, can see all sides of a muscle and how it moves. [5]Finally, viewers will be able to interact with materials by typing in critical comments, updating information, and even changing the outcome of a story.

___ 3. [1]A major study of firstborn children reveals that they tend to be super-achievers who strive very hard to make their families proud. [2]It was discovered that of the country's first twenty-three astronauts, an amazing twenty-one were firstborn in their families. [3]Also, slightly more than half—52 percent—of our presidents were firstborn children. [4]Less positive is the fact that firstborns are under a lot of pressure to succeed, because their families often pin their hopes and dreams on them. [5]Also, as the eldest, they are expected to "set an example" for their younger brothers and sisters. [6]Furthermore, these firstborns sometimes have trouble with personal relationships because they learned to be very independent and to enjoy doing things on their own—since they were the only children in their families until their younger brothers and sisters were born. [7]The conclusion of the study is that being a firstborn child is a mixed blessing, having positive as well as some negative aspects.

(Continues on next page)

___ 4. [1]Unlike many lower animals that use their noses to detect mates, predators, and prey, humans do not depend on their sense of smell for survival. [2]Nevertheless, the sense of smell in humans is incredibly sensitive. [3]Only a few molecules of a substance reaching the smell receptors are necessary to cause humans to perceive an odor. [4]Certain substances can be detected in especially small amounts. [5]Decayed cabbage, lemons, and rotten eggs are examples. [6]So too is mercaptan, a foul-smelling substance added to natural gas that we can smell in concentrations as small as one part per fifty billion parts of air. [7]According to one estimate, the sense of smell is about ten thousand times more sensitive than that of taste.

___ 5. [1]At the outset of the nineteenth century, there was a lack of reliable, comfortable travel. [2]The stagecoach was the major form of transportation. [3]Twelve passengers, crowded along with their bags and parcels, traveled at just four miles an hour. [4]Wretched roads plagued travelers. [5]Larger towns had roads paved with cobblestones; potholes in major highways were filled with stones. [6]Most roads were simply dirt paths. [7]Rain left these roads muddy and rutted. [8]The presence of tree stumps in the middle of many roads posed a serious obstacle to carriages.

MAIN IDEAS: Test D

The following paragraphs have main ideas (topic sentences) that may appear at any place within the paragraph. Identify the topic sentence of each paragraph by filling in the correct sentence number in the space provided.

____ 1. ¹The personalities of adopted children do not much resemble those of their adoptive parents. ²Studies show, however, that adoptive parents do have many generally positive effects on their children. ³First, the home environment influences adopted children's values, beliefs, and social attitudes. ⁴Second, in adoptive homes, child neglect and abuse are rare. ⁵Adopted children are less than half as likely as other children to have divorced or separated parents. ⁶Adoptive parents are carefully screened; natural parents are not. ⁷So it is not surprising that nearly all adopted children thrive. ⁸They score higher than their biological parents on intelligence tests, and many become happier and more stable people than they would have in a stressed or neglectful environment.

____ 2. ¹Self-serving bonds exist between unrelated members of the animal kingdom. ²Take the leopard and the battler eagle, for instance. ³A leopard will go to any lengths to keep other animals from its kill, even to the point of storing the carcass high above the ground in the fork of a tree. ⁴But the leopard enters into a firm partnership with the battler eagle who, in return for a share of the meat, guards the kill and warns the cat of potential poachers. ⁵Or consider the rhinoceros and its flocks of tickbirds and egrets. ⁶The rhino, nearly blind, relies on the birds' eyesight to warn it of approaching danger while the birds fill themselves up on the host of ticks and other parasites infecting the rhino's hide. ⁷Even in the ocean, these beneficial relationships flourish. ⁸Moray eels and cleaner fish, for example, peacefully inhabit the same reef. ⁹The cleaner fish get an all-you-can-eat dinner on the eel's parasites, and the eel receives a free grooming session.

____ 3. ¹Imagine a successful fisherman who needs a new sail for his boat. ²In a barter economy—that is, one in which goods are exchanged directly for one another—he would have to find someone who not only needs fish but is willing to exchange a sail for it. ³If no sailmaker wants fish, the fisherman must find someone else—say, a shoemaker—who wants fish and will trade for it. ⁴The fisherman must hope that the sailmaker will trade for the shoes. ⁵In a money economy, the fisherman would sell his catch, receive money, and exchange the money for such goods as a new sail. ⁶Clearly, barter is quite inefficient in comparison to money.

(Continues on next page)

___ 4. [1]Your sleep style is at least partly influenced by your personality and your gender. [2]According to Army research, people who are very sociable and physically active tend to be "short" sleepers (those who require six or fewer hours of sleep to feel refreshed). [3]Folks who are mainly introverted and mentally creative are more likely to be "long" sleepers (those who need more than eight hours). [4]It's thought that these people, because of the extra time they spend "in their head," are more aware of themselves and their inner conflicts than very social or physically oriented people might be. [5]And since dreams offer us an opportunity to work out problems, they need and use the extra dream time to resolve mental conflicts and puzzles. [6]The researchers further noted that women tend to awaken more frequently than men do and to sleep less soundly, as well. [7]It is speculated that the reason for this is biochemical, since women, through most stages of life, experience greater hormonal shifts than men do.

___ 5. [1]In Western society, adolescence is an often stormy period that frequently places parents and their children in conflict. [2]Adolescents are told to "act like adults," but they are often treated as children. [3]The Mbuti tribe of East Africa provides a practical solution to the problem of how to become an adult. [4]Mbuti boys and girls are taken from their homes to separate "marriage and adulthood" camps. [5]During the three months that the camps last, the children are taught about the responsibilities of adulthood. [6]They learn about sharing, conflict, and respecting others. [7]The elders of the community talk to them about spiritual and moral values. [8]When the "campers" return to their village, they are no longer boys and girls. [9]They are men and women entitled to marry and set up their own homes.

SUPPORTING DETAILS: Test A

A. Answer the questions or follow the directions for the textbook passages below.

[1]Stereotyping consists of assigning traits to people solely on the basis of a category. [2]Some researchers suggest that stereotyping has four clear phases. [3]First, a person distinguishes some category of people, for example, economists. [4]Second, the person notes that one or more of the people in this category have certain traits, for example, dullness. [5]Third, the person generalizes that everyone in this category has these characteristics, for example, that all economists are dull. [6]Finally, when meeting someone the person is not acquainted with but knows to be, for example, an economist, the person stereotypes this individual as dull.

____ 1. In general, the major supporting details of this paragraph are
   A. characteristics given to people solely on the basis of their class or category.
   B. people who have studied stereotypes.
   C. examples of stereotyping.
   D. the stages people go through when they stereotype.

____ 2. How many major details are in this paragraph?
   A. Two
   B. Three
   C. Four
   D. Five

____ 3. Sentence 2 provides
   A. the main idea.
   B. a major detail.
   C. a minor detail.

____ 4. Economists are used in the paragraph as
   A. the main idea.
   B. major details.
   C. minor details.

____ 5. According to some researchers, people who stereotype end up by judging
   A. phases.
   B. friends.
   C. acquaintances.
   D. individuals they are not acquainted with.

(Continues on next page)

[1]There are three principal kinds of animal diets. [2]In a carnivorous diet, animals feed on other animals. [3]Most fish are carnivorous. [4]So too are owls, snakes, and wolves. [5]On an herbivorous diet, animals subsist on plant food. [6]Cattle, Japanese beetles, seed-eating birds, and plant lice are among the many herbivores. [7]With the omnivorous diet, animals have a mixed diet. [8]They feed on both vegetable and animal matter, dead or alive. [9]Many kinds of worms, crabs, lobsters, insects, bears and raccoons are omnivorous. [10]Humans are also omnivores.

6. Complete the outline of the paragraph by filling in the missing major detail.

Principal kinds of animal diets.

1. Carnivorous (animals)

2. _____

3. Omnivorous (animals and plants)

B. (7–10.) Complete the outline of the following paragraph by filling in the rest of the main idea and the major supporting details, including an explanation of each. One explanation has been done for you.

[1]Burn injuries are classified in three categories, according to their severity. [2]First-degree burns are burns that leave a painful red mark but do not break the skin, and thus they do not often become infected. [3]Burns that are classified as second-degree burn through the skin, which develops blisters. [4]Second-degree burns are often extremely painful, and, since the skin has been broken, they may become infected. [5]In a third-degree burn, both the outer layer and lower layer of skin are burned. [6]There may be little pain because nerve endings have been destroyed. [7]Because so much of the skin's protection has been lost, the possibility of serious, even fatal infection is great with a third-degree burn.

Main idea: There are three _____

_____

1. _____

_____

2. _____—burn through skin, causing blisters

and often great pain and infection

3. _____

_____

SUPPORTING DETAILS: Test B

A. Answer the questions that follow the passage.

[1]Self-disclosure is a special type of conversation in which we share intimate information and feelings with another person. [2]There are many reasons why we disclose personal information to another person. [3]One is simply to express our feelings—to "get them off our chest." [4]After a hard day at work, we may eagerly tell a friend just how angry we are at our boss and how unappreciated we feel. [5]A second reason for self-disclosure is to gain greater understanding and self-awareness. [6]Talking to a friend about a problem can help us to clarify our thoughts about the situation. [7]Social approval is another reason for disclosing information. [8]By seeing how a listener reacts to what we say, we get information about the appropriateness of our views. [9]People may reassure us that our reactions are "perfectly normal" or suggest that we're "blowing things out of proportion." [10]Yet another common reason for self-disclosure is relationship development. [11]The sharing of personal information is an important way to begin a relationship and to move toward increasing levels of intimacy.

____ 1. The main idea is expressed in
   A. sentence 1.
   B. sentence 2.
   C. sentence 3.
   D. sentence 11.

____ 2. In general, the major details of the passage are
   A. ways to express our feelings.
   B. thoughts about the appropriateness of our views.
   C. ways to begin relationships.
   D. reasons we disclose information to others.

____ 3. How many major details are in this paragraph?
   A. Two
   B. Three
   C. Four
   D. Five

____ 4. The first major detail is introduced with the addition word
   A. *another.*
   B. *many.*
   C. *one.*
   D. *other.*

____ 5. Self-disclosure is a conversation in which
   A. we discuss anything of interest.
   B. our reactions are blown out of proportion.
   C. we share something personal.
   D. we discuss social approval.

(Continues on next page)

B. (6–10.) Complete the outline of the following paragraph by filling in the rest of the main idea and the missing major and minor supporting details.

¹Although the debate continues over how important heredity is versus environment, scientists have learned that a number of human characteristics clearly have genetic factors. ²Physical traits are most strongly determined by heredity. ³Height, obesity, and patterns of tooth decay are just a few of the traits that have been found to be determined by our genes. ⁴Intellectual traits are also strongly influenced by genes. ⁵For instance, research indicates that scores on intelligence tests and memory have a strong hereditary basis. ⁶In addition, personality factors are greatly influenced by heredity. ⁷Shyness and special talents and interests are all influenced by genetic transmission. ⁸Even emotional disorders such as schizophrenia are affected by genes.

Main idea: A number of human characteristics have _____

    1. Physical traits

      Examples—height, obesity, and patterns of tooth decay

    2. _____

      Examples— _____

    3. _____

      Examples— _____

    4. Emotional disorders

      Example—schizophrenia

Name _____

Section _____ Date _____

SCORE: (Number correct) × 10 = _____%

SUPPORTING DETAILS: Test C

A. (1–4.) Complete the map of the following textbook passage by filling in the main idea and the three missing major details, including an explanation of each. One explanation has been started for you.

[1]Psychologists use several theories to explain different sides of human behavior. [2]Best-known is the psychoanalytic theory, which holds that people are driven largely by needs and desires that they are not aware of—the so-called "subconscious" mind. [3]Another theory, behaviorism, suggests that people's actions are based largely on past experiences of reward and punishment. [4]We do things that brought us pleasant results in the past and avoid things that brought unpleasant results. [5]Yet another theory, "gestalt" psychology, emphasizes the role of overall patterns in our thinking. [6]For example, we find it much easier to remember a tune than a series of unconnected musical notes.

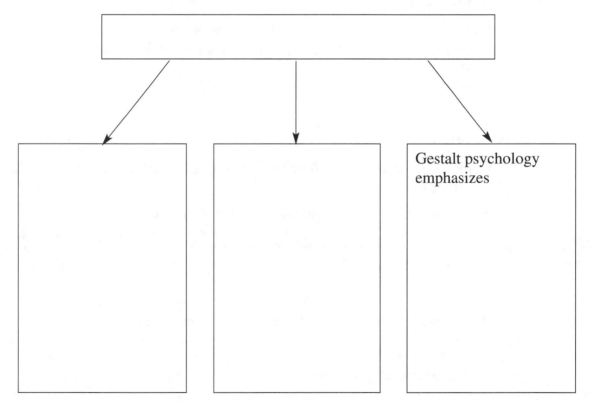

Gestalt psychology emphasizes

(Continues on next page)

B. Carefully read the paragraph, and then answer the questions that follow.

¹People once thought that the mountains, plains, plateaus, and other features of the Earth had always existed. ²But the science of geology reveals that two processes work continuously to shape and to alter the face of the Earth: the forces of construction and the forces of destruction. ³The constructive forces are those that lift up the land masses to produce forms like mountains. ⁴Earthquakes and volcanoes demonstrate the workings of constructive forces. ⁵The destructive forces are those which cause the leveling down of mountains and hills. ⁶The cutting action of running streams and the rubbing of glacial ice are some of the forces that reduce the high places of the Earth.

___ 5. The main idea of the passage is expressed in sentence number _____.

___ 6. In general, the major details of this paragraph are
  A. geological features of the Earth.
  B. processes that shape and alter the face of the Earth.
  C. features of the Earth.
  D. the high places on Earth.

___ 7. Specifically, the major details of this paragraph are
  A. mountains, plains, plateaus, and other features of the Earth.
  B. shaping and altering.
  C. the Earth's constructive forces and destructive forces.
  D. earthquakes and volcanoes.

___ 8. Mountains are produced by the Earth's _____ forces.

9–10. Complete the following outline of the paragraph by filling in the missing major and minor supporting details.

Two processes that shape and alter the face of the Earth

  1. _____

    a. Earthquakes

    b. Volcanoes

  2. Destructive forces, which level down mountains and hills

    a. _____

    b. Rubbing of glacial ice

SUPPORTING DETAILS: Test D

A. (1–6.) Complete the map of the following paragraph by filling in the main idea and the five major supporting details.

¹A number of factors contribute to the fact that poor people are less healthy than well-off people. ²For one thing, low-income families tend to have less nutritious diets than higher-income families. ³In particular, low-income diets are often deficient in the amount of protein which they provide. ⁴Many poorer families probably have some level of malnutrition much of the time, a fact that influences their susceptibility to illness. ⁵Second, the general standard of living among low-income groups is likely to be lower. ⁶Their homes are more crowded, more likely to be in disrepair, and more often located in dangerous neighborhoods. ⁷Another factor affecting health in poor people is that low-income families usually receive less medical care and lower-quality medical care than wealthier ones do. ⁸Failure to have minor ailments cared for may make these people more likely to have major ailments later on. ⁹Fourth, people with low incomes are probably under a lot of physical stress, a factor which appears to be related to the onset of illness. ¹⁰Last of all, poor people are subject to a great deal of psychological stress, a factor that may be even more powerful than physical stress in leaving the body exposed to illness.

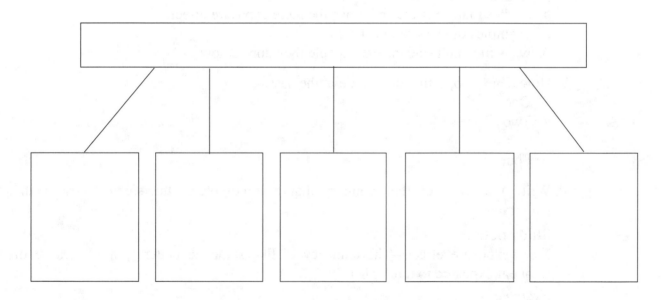

(Continues on next page)

B. After reading the textbook passage below, answer the questions or follow the directions.

     [1]The *mere exposure effect*—the tendency to like someone better simply because of frequent exposure to him or her—has been observed in studies. [2]In one study, college students were shown pictures of faces. [3]Some of the faces were shown as many as twenty-five times, others only once or twice. [4]Afterward, subjects indicated how much they liked each face and how much they thought they would like the person pictured. [5]The more often the subjects had seen a face, the more they said they liked it and thought they would like the person. [6]The same result has been found for repeated exposure to actual people. [7]In a recent study, researchers enlisted the aid of four college women who served as confederates in an experiment. [8]A pretest showed that all women were rated as equally attractive. [9]In the study, each woman attended a large lecture class in social psychology, posing as a student in the course. [10]Each woman attended a different number of class sessions—once, five times, ten times, or fifteen times during the term. [11]At the end of the term, students in the class were asked to rate each woman, based on a casual photo shown as a slide. [12]The more often students had seen a woman, the more they thought they would like her.

7. *Fill in the blank:* The main idea of the paragraph is expressed in sentence
_____.

___ 8. The supporting details are
    A. reasons to like someone.
    B. studies that illustrate and prove the mere exposure effect.
    C. examples of classroom behavior.
    D. ways in which students rate people they don't know.

___ 9. How many supporting details are in the passage?
    A. One
    B. Two
    C. Three
    D. Four

___10. Write the letter of the summary that best completes the study notes of the paragraph.

Study notes:

Mere exposure effect—The tendency to like someone better simply because of frequent exposure to him or her

Example—
    A. In one study, college students were shown pictures of faces, some as many as twenty-five times.
    B. The more often students saw each of four women in their class, the more they thought they would like her.
    C. Four women who were rated as equally attractive attended a large lecture class once, five, ten, or fifteen times during the term.

IMPLIED MAIN IDEAS/CENTRAL POINT: Test A

A. In the space provided, write the letter of the sentence that best expresses the implied main idea of each of the following paragraphs.

___ 1. [1]A puddle of dark liquid under a car indicates a leak in the oil or transmission fluid. [2]Another warning sign of car trouble is uneven wear on tire treads. [3]If the outer edge of the tire tread wears out before the center, the tire is under-inflated. [4]The most significant early warning signal, however, is less and less mileage per gallon. [5]Lower fuel economy is caused by a variety of problems ranging from a clogged filter to ignition or carburetor trouble.

    A. Several warning signs can indicate car problems.
    B. A puddle of dark liquid under a car is a sign that a car has an oil or transmission-fluid leak.
    C. The most significant warning signal of a car problem is getting lower mileage per gallon of gas.
    D. Various problems may cause a car's fuel economy to decrease.

___ 2. [1]We think of crime as having a clear victim who suffers at the hands of another person. [2]Some crimes, however, don't seem to have victims. [3]These victimless crimes include prostitution, illicit drug use, and gambling. [4]In this type of crime, there is usually no one who feels he or she has been harmed. [5]These acts are called criminal because the community as a whole, or powerful groups within it, regard them as morally wrong. [6]Those who hold different views of morality think that at least some of these behaviors should not be considered criminal. [7]Still others argue that victimless crimes really do have victims. [8]For example, compulsive gamblers rob their families of income. [9]Also, prostitutes spread AIDS and other sexually transmitted diseases, and drug users may resort to other crimes to support their habit.

    A. Victimless activities such as prostitution and gambling should not be illegal.
    B. The community or a powerful part of it determines what activities are criminal.
    C. There are varying views of victimless crimes.
    D. One view of victimless crimes is that they in fact do have victims.

___ 3. [1]A round foundation in Africa that is two million years old reveals an appreciation like our own for balance and form. [2]A flower arrangement found in an ancient burial site in Iraq suggests that flowers were a symbol of comfort. [3]Ice Age sculptures emphasize human sexuality, showing the importance of fertility to early people. [4]And cave paintings dating back to 20,000 B.C. prove that the artists were keen observers of nature.

    A. Ancient artists were even more talented than artists of recent centuries.
    B. Early human handiwork suggests that ancient peoples had values and sensitivities much like our own.
    C. An ancient flower arrangement at a burial site shows that flowers have been a symbol of comfort for centuries.
    D. Humans were interested in producing art as far back as 20,000 B.C.

(Continues on next page)

B. (4.) The author has stated the central point of the following textbook selection in one sentence. Find and underline that sentence. Then, in the space provided, write the number of the sentence that contains the central point.

America in 1901

[1]As the nation reached adulthood, a number of ugly problems existed. [2]Maldistribution of wealth and income persisted. [3]One percent of American families possessed nearly seven-eighths of its wealth. [4]Four-fifths of Americans lived on a survival level while a handful lived in incredible luxury. [5]In 1900, Andrew Carnegie earned about $23 million; the average working man earned $500. [6]The wealth of a few was increased by the exploitation of women and children. [7]One out of five women worked for food rather than fulfillment, earning wages as low as $6 a week. [8]The sacrifice of the country's young to the god of economic growth was alarming. [9]One reporter undertook to do a child's job in the mines for one day and wrote, "I tried to pick out the pieces of slate from the hurrying stream of coal, often missing them; my hands were bruised and cut within a few minutes; I was covered from head to foot with coal dust, and for many hours afterwards I was expectorating some of the small particles of anthracite I had swallowed."

[10]Working conditions were equally horrifying in other industries, and for many Americans, housing conditions were as bad or worse. [11]One investigator described a Chicago neighborhood, remarking on the "filthy and rotten tenements, the dingy courts and tumbledown sheds, the foul stables and dilapidated outhouses, the broken sewer pipes, and piles of garbage fairly alive with diseased odors." [12]At the same time, the Vanderbilts summered in a "cottage" of seventy rooms, and wealthy men partied in shirts with diamond buttons worth thousands of dollars.

[13]The middle class experienced neither extreme. [14]Its members did have their economic grievances, however. [15]Prosperity increased the cost of living by 35 percent in less than a decade while many middle-class incomes remained fairly stable. [16]Such people were not poor, but they believed they were not getting a fair share of the prosperity.

_____ is the number of the sentence that states the central point.

IMPLIED MAIN IDEAS/CENTRAL POINT: Test B

A. Write the letter of the sentence that best expresses the implied main idea of each of the following paragraphs.

1. ¹In the late 1980s, concern about the deadly effects of illegal drugs became a top national issue. ²Politicians loudly proclaimed a "war on drugs," and TV news shows carried regular reports about the fatal toll of drugs, especially "crack" cocaine. ³These drugs do have a terrible effect on individuals and society, but the facts about them are somewhat different from their popular image. ⁴Each year, about two thousand people die from heroin overdoses, and about three thousand die from cocaine-related causes. ⁵At the same time, 50,000 people die every year because of alcohol—including thousands of innocent victims of drunk drivers. ⁶Additionally, a third of a million people die every year from cancer due to smoking cigarettes.

   A. In the late 1980s, politicians proclaimed a "war on drugs."
   B. Our "war on drugs" ignores the two deadliest (though legal) drugs, alcohol and tobacco.
   C. Thousands of people die each year from heroin overdoses and cocaine-related causes.
   D. More people die each year from alcohol-related causes than from cocaine-related causes.

2. ¹One reason tabloids publish untrue stories about celebrities, even though they know the celebrities might sue, is free advertising. ²If there is a lawsuit, it will make the news, and the tabloid gains the publicity. ³Furthermore, in a lawsuit the burden of proof is on the celebrity, not the paper. ⁴Also, such lawsuits are both expensive and time-consuming. ⁵A court delay, for example, can prevent a movie star from beginning work on a new project. ⁶And the chances of collecting a significant amount of damages are slim. ⁷Finally, tabloids publish untrue stories for the obvious reason: whether it is true or not, people love celebrity gossip—and it sells papers.

   a. Tabloids publish untrue stories about celebrities.
   b. Tabloids publish untrue stories about celebrities because celebrities will think twice about suing.
   c. There are a few reasons why tabloids publish untrue stories about celebrities even though the celebrities might sue.
   d. Even if celebrities sue tabloids over untrue stories, they are unlikely to collect a lot of money for damages.

3. ¹In the past it often took years to force a car company to make even small, inexpensive changes. ²In the 1960s, consumer advocate Ralph Nader had to fight for several years before Chevrolet stopped making the unsafe Corvair. ³But in recent years, customer complaints and publicity have led to quick corrective actions. ⁴For example, the Consumers Union recently reported that all-terrain

(Continues on next page)

vehicles (ATVs) were unsafe when driven by untrained operators. ⁵Within eighteen months, ATV makers stopped making unstable three-wheeled models and set up an extensive customer training program. ⁶More recently, *Consumer Reports* magazine revealed safety problems in the Ford Bronco II. ⁷In response, Ford immediately announced a complete redesign and plans to market the re-engineered vehicle under a new name.

A. Companies should respond more quickly to changes demanded by consumer advocates.
B. Ralph Nader had to fight for years in the 1960s before Chevrolet stopped making the unsafe Corvair.
C. Because of customer complains and publicity, car manufacturers are correcting car problems more quickly than they once did.
D. If you want a product to be improved, take the responsibility of complaining to the company.

B. (4.) The author has stated the central point of the following textbook selection in one sentence. Find and underline that sentence. Then, in the space provided, write the number of the sentence that contains the central point.

Arranged Marriages

¹Our culture places a high premium on personal choice in matters of the heart. ²In contrast, many traditional societies throughout the world reject individual choice and romance as a basis for marriage. ³In parts of India, for example, marriages are arranged by parents. ⁴Love is not viewed as an important basis for marriage there. ⁵When parents select a bride, they emphasize her good character, obedience, domestic skills, religiousness, and appearance. ⁶In selecting a groom, the social and economic standing of the family and the young man's education and earning potential are paramount.

⁷Teenagers who grow up in traditional societies often welcome their parents' help in selecting a mate. ⁸When girls in India learned about American marriage customs, they expressed serious concerns about the hazards of free choice. ⁹One girl asked if an American girl who is shy and does not call attention to herself might not get married. ¹⁰Another girl said it would be humiliating to have to attract a boy. ¹¹"It makes getting married a sort of competition in which the girls are fighting each other for the boys. ¹²And it encourages a girl to pretend she's better than she really is." ¹³Other girls praised their parents' judgment about a potential husband. ¹⁴"It's so important that the man I marry should be the right one. ¹⁵I could so easily make a mistake if I had to find him for myself."

¹⁶An anthropologist has painted a similar portrait of marriage in traditional Chinese culture. ¹⁷For centuries, it was common for Chinese marriages to be arranged by parents and hired go-betweens; the partners might not even meet until their wedding. ¹⁸Proponents of arranged marriage emphasize that parents are better judges of character than children and that passion is an unrealistic basis for marriage. ¹⁹They observe that well-matched partners from compatible families gradually learn to find love and satisfaction with each other.

_____ is the number of the sentence that states the central point.

IMPLIED MAIN IDEAS/CENTRAL POINT: Test C

A. Write the letter of the sentence that best expresses the implied main idea of each of the following passages.

1. [1]During the 1989 Northern California earthquake, a half-mile section of elevated freeway in Oakland collapsed on itself. [2]Since the earthquake happened right at the afternoon rush hour, early estimates were that more than two hundred people might have died, crushed in the rubble. [3]But by sheer good luck, the earthquake came just before the scheduled start of a World Series baseball game between the Oakland "A's" and the San Francisco Giants. [4]Thousands of people had left work early to get home for the game. [5]Others went to friends' homes or bars near where they worked to watch the game, instead of driving straight home. [6]Thus, few people were on the freeway when the quake hit, and the death toll was much lower than expected.

   A. The 1989 Northern California earthquake came just before the scheduled start of a World Series game.
   B. Because of a scheduled World Series game, the death toll from the 1989 Northern California earthquake was lower than expected.
   C. Being on the freeway during an earthquake is more dangerous than being at home.
   D. Before the 1989 Northern California earthquake, many people left work early to watch the World Series.

2. [1]How much water is stored as glacial ice? [2]Estimates by the U.S. geological survey indicate that only slightly more than 2 percent of the world's water is accounted for by glaciers. [3]But this small figure may be misleading when the actual amounts of water are considered. [4]The total volume of all valley glaciers is about 210,000 cubic kilometers. [5]That volume is comparable to the combined volume of the world's largest saltwater and freshwater lakes. [6]Furthermore, 80 percent of the world's ice and nearly two-thirds of the Earth's fresh water are represented by Antarctica's ice sheet, which covers an area almost one and one-half times that of the United States. [7]If this ice melted, sea level would rise an estimated sixty to seventy meters, and the ocean would flood many densely populated coastal areas. [8]The amount of the continent's ice can be illustrated in another way. [9]If Antarctica's ice sheet were melted at a uniform rate, it would feed (1) the Mississippi River for more than 50,000 years, (2) all the rivers in the United States for about 17,000 years, (3) the Amazon River for approximately 5,000 years, or (4) all the rivers of the world for about 750 years.

   A. If melted at a uniform rate, Antarctica's ice sheet would feed the Mississippi River for 50,000 years.
   B. The world's water takes various forms—salt water, fresh water, and ice.
   C. If Antarctica's glacial ice were melted, the ocean would flood many heavily populated coastal areas.
   D. The quantity of glacial ice on Earth today is truly immense.

(Continues on next page)

B. (3.) Write out the implied main idea of the following paragraph.

    [1]Some researchers have found that women are more likely than men to use eye contact and smiles to attract members of the opposite sex. [2]Women also have a tendency to use fleeting touches and seductive grooming, such as lip licking and hair smoothing, as flirting signals. [3]In comparison, men rarely make these gestures for the same purpose. [4]Indeed, according to the researchers, the only flirting technique that men use frequently is the obvious, direct approach—hugging or kissing, which is as direct as you can get!

Implied main idea: _____

_____

C. (4.) The author has stated the central point of the following textbook selection in one sentence. Find and underline that sentence. Then, in the space provided, write the number of the sentence that contains the central point.

Happiness

    [1]In their research on happiness, psychologists have studied influences upon both our temporary moods and our long-term life satisfaction. [2]Studying people's reports of daily moods confirms that stressful events—an argument, a sick child, a car problem—trigger bad moods. [3]No surprise there. [4]But by the next day, the gloom nearly always lifts. [5]When in a bad mood, can you usually depend on rebounding within a day or two? [6]Are your times of joy hard to keep going? [7]Research psychologists have learned that in the long run, our emotional ups and downs tend to wear off, and we go back to feeling as we always did.

    [8]Apart from prolonged grief over the loss of a loved one or continuing anxiety after a traumatic stress, such as child abuse, rape, or the terrors of war, even tragedy is not permanently depressing. [9]The finding is surprising but reliable. [10]People who become blind or paralyzed usually recover near-normal levels of day-to-day happiness. [11]For example, able-bodied University of Illinois students described themselves as happy 50 percent of the time, unhappy 22 percent of the time, and neutral 29 percent of the time. [12]To within one percentage point, students with disabilities rated their emotions identically. [13]Moreover, students perceive their friends with disabilities as just as happy as their other friends.

    [14]The effect of dramatically positive events is similarly temporary. [15]Once the rush of euphoria wears off, state lottery winners typically find their overall happiness is unchanged. [16]Other research confirms that there is much more to well-being than being well-off. [17]Many people believe they would be happier if they had more money. [18]They probably would be—temporarily. [19]But in the long run, increased wealth hardly affects happiness. [20]People with lots of money are not much happier than those with just enough money to afford life's necessities.

_____ is the number of the sentence that states the central point.

IMPLIED MAIN IDEAS/CENTRAL POINT: Test D

A. Write the letter of the sentence that best expresses the implied main idea of each of the following textbook paragraphs.

1. [1]Many companies sell tapes with subliminal messages, messages that are too faint to consciously hear. [2]The companies promise that the tapes will "reprogram your unconscious mind for success and happiness." [3]Is there anything to these wild claims? [4]Some researchers decided to find out. [5]They randomly assigned eager university students to listen daily for five weeks to commercial subliminal tapes designed to improve either self-esteem or memory. [6]On half the tapes the researchers switched the labels. [7]People given these tapes thought they were receiving statements supporting self-esteem, when they actually heard the memory enhancement tape. [8]Or they got the memory tape but thought their self-esteem was being recharged. [9]Were the tapes effective? [10]Scores on both self-esteem and memory tests, taken before and after the five weeks, revealed no effects at all.

   A. According to one study, subliminal tapes that are sold with promises of self-improvement have no effects at all.
   B. University students were assigned to listen to commercial subliminal tapes daily for five weeks.
   C. Companies claim that subliminal tapes can positively influence one's success and happiness.
   D. Many products do not live up to the claims made for them.

2. [1]The University of California at Santa Cruz wanted undergraduates to conserve water by taking shorter showers. [2]So they posted signs in the men's shower rooms urging bathers to "(1) wet down, (2) turn water off, (3) soap up, (4) rinse off." [3]But only 6 percent of students complied with the posted request. [4]A psychologist used conformity pressure to improve matters dramatically. [5]He had an assistant wait in the shower room, poised to take a shower, until a student entered the room. [6]Then the assistant showered, carefully following the instructions on the sign. [7]Nearly half the students who encountered this energy-conscious assistant followed the recommended procedures. [8]When there were two water-saving assistants, compliance by students increased to 67 percent.

   A. A sign telling university students how to shower in order to conserve water was largely ignored.
   B. All too often, signs asking for cooperation have little influence on citizens.
   C. A good way of achieving the important goal of conserving water is to take shorter showers.
   D. Conformity pressure did a much better job of getting students to conserve water than a sign alone did.

(Continues on next page)

B. (3.) Write out the implied main idea of the following paragraph.

¹Scientists have wondered for years how the monarch butterfly, an insect with a brain the size of a pinhead, can migrate almost two thousand miles from various points in North America to winter in California and Mexico. ²To complicate the mystery, because of the monarch's short life span, the butterflies who migrate in the fall are a few generations removed from the ones who did it the year before. ³Therefore, each monarch makes the journey home without the benefit of memory. ⁴One more puzzling aspect of this insect has intrigued scientists throughout their studies: Out of all the butterflies in the world, the monarch is the only type that migrates.

Implied main idea: _____

_____

C. (4.) The author has stated the central point of the following textbook selection in one sentence. Find and underline that sentence. Then, in the space provided, write the number of the sentence that contains the central point.

Judging Risks

¹With horrific television and magazine images of air crashes in mind, many people prefer the safety of their own cars. ²Of those who do fly, 44 percent report feeling fearful.

³Ironically, the reality is that, mile for mile, U.S. travelers during the 1980s were twenty-six times more likely to die in a car crash than on a commercial flight. ⁴In one study in the 1990s, major U.S. airlines carried more than one billion passengers on sixteen million flights without a single death. ⁵For most air travelers, the most dangerous part of the journey is the drive to the airport.

⁶Similarly, many people are likely to exaggerate the likelihood of shark attacks after watching the film *Jaws*, which was about a killer shark. ⁷Or from seeing the faces of missing children on milk cartons, people may misjudge their child's risk of being abducted by a stranger. ⁸The U.S. Justice Department reports that fewer than 1 in 100,000 children a year nationwide are abducted. ⁹(Almost all child snatchings are family-related.)

¹⁰In 2001, the terrorist attacks in hijacked planes on the World Trade Center and the Pentagon caused many would-be international vacationers to stay home and brave dangerous highways instead. ¹¹The same fearful public continues to drive without seatbelts, smoke billions of cigarettes a year, guzzle alcohol, and devour foods that put people at risk for the greatest of killers—heart disease. ¹²Also, while the public dreads a horrible nuclear accident (which after the 1986 Chernobyl disaster we can readily visualize), it accepts the less dramatic risk of coal-generated power, which quietly fuels acid rain and global warming.

¹³Whether making travel plans or choosing foods, defining safety standards or evaluating environmental hazards, people often judge risks based on media images, not on statistical reality.

_____ is the number of the sentence that states the central point.

RELATIONSHIPS I: Test A

A. Fill in each blank with the appropriate transition word from the box. Use each transition once.

after	also	another
next	until	

1. ¹Abraham Lincoln grew a beard only _____ being elected to the presidency. ²An eleven-year-old girl told him that with a beard he "would look a great deal better, for your face is so thin."

2. ¹Tina's father is an overly cautious parent. ²He wants to know where she is every minute, and he won't let her drive his car _____ she is 20.

3. ¹In 1835 Halley's comet appeared and Mark Twain was born. ²Twain predicted that he'd die when Halley's comet showed up again. ³And he did die in 1910, the year of the comet's _____ appearance.

4. ¹Other boys like to collect normal things, like baseball cards, but my little brother Dwayne collects dead bugs. ²He _____ collects loose chunks of sidewalk (which he insists on calling moon rocks).

5. ¹There have been many fictional captains. ²One is Captain Marvel, the red-suited comic-strip superhero. ³_____ is Captain Nemo, captain of the submarine in Jules Verne's *Twenty Thousand Leagues Under the Sea*.

(Continues on next page)

B. Fill in each blank with an appropriate transition word from the box. Use each transition once. Then answer the question that follows.

another	during	one
third		

[1]Many people who do sit-ups may not be getting the full benefit of the exercise because they're doing them incorrectly. [2]Here are three common sit-up errors—and what should be done instead. [3](6)_____ error is allowing the stomach muscles to bulge out, rather than tucking them in. [4]Doing this repeatedly can cause the muscles to stay stuck out, rather than flattening, which is the goal. [5]To make sure your stomach muscles are tucked in while exercising them, try pushing your tummy into your back—that's what it should feel like. [6](7)_____ error is not breathing while doing sit-ups. [7]Many people instinctively hold their breath during physical exertion—so they don't get the oxygen necessary to fuel an effective workout. [8]The proper (and easiest) way to breathe (8)_____ sit-ups is to inhale for the easy part (lowering your back) and then to exhale during the hard part (lifting yourself up). [9]A (9)_____ error is keeping the legs straight, which uses—and can strain—the lower-back muscles, rather than making full use of the stomach muscles. [10]For safer, more effective sit-ups, keep those knees bent.

10. The main pattern of organization of the above paragraph is
    A. list of items.
    B. time order.

RELATIONSHIPS I: Test B

A. Write the letter of the answer that describes the relationship indicated by the italicized transition.

1. *After* the magician's assistant shuts the closet door, the magician escapes from the closet through a door in the floor.

   The relationship of the first part of the sentence to the second part is one of
   A. addition.   B. time.

2. It's impossible to do everything perfectly, and *moreover,* it's ridiculous to try.

   The relationship of the second part of the sentence to the first part is one of
   A. addition.   B. time.

3. First the pinch hitter selected a bat from the rack. *Then* he took a few practice swings.

   The relationship of the second sentence to the first is one of
   A. addition.   B. time.

4. You can use various methods to get your listeners' attention. *For one thing,* you can tell a joke or an anecdote.

   The relationship of the second sentence to the first is one of
   A. addition.   B. time.

5. Emotions have a physical basis in our hormone system. They are *also* grounded in our experience.

   The relationship of the second sentence to the first is one of
   A. addition.   B. time.

B. Read the passage and answer the question that follows.

> [1]The vocabulary of a society or a group tells us what kinds of things are important to it. [2]First of all, sociologists have often noted that although most of us think and speak only of "snow" and "ice," the Eskimos, or Inuit, have many different words for them—depending on whether snow is freshly fallen and fluffy or old and packed down, or hard or melting, and on whether ice is solid or cracking. [3]Skiers also have many terms for snow, and skaters speak (with awe) of "black ice." [4]Clearly, snow and ice are important to these groups. [5]As a final example, people in the nineteenth century had many terms for a horse-drawn vehicle: buggy, dogcart, hansom, barouche, landau, phaeton, and more. [6]These carriages were an important aspect of their world, though today the terms mean little to us—we have many terms, instead, for automobiles.

6. The main pattern of organization of the paragraph is
   A. list of items.
   B. time order.

(Continues on next page)

C. Fill in each blank with an appropriate transition word from the box. Use each transition once. Then answer the question that follows.

as	finally	then

[1]A calorie is the amount of heat required to raise the temperature of a kilogram (about a quart) of water one degree Celsius. [2]To determine the number of calories in a portion of food, a technician uses a device called a bomb calorimeter. [3]This device has a chamber that rests in a container of water. [4]The food is placed in this chamber, which is (7)_____ filled with oxygen under high pressure. [5]Next, the food is set on fire. [6](8)_____ it burns, it gives off heat, and the temperature of the water in the container rises. [7](9)_____, the total rise in temperature is measured, giving the calorie content of the food.

10. The main pattern of organization of the paragraph is
    A. list of items.
    B. time order.

Name _____

Section _____ Date _____

SCORE: (Number correct) × 10 = _____%

RELATIONSHIPS I: Test C

Read each textbook passage and answer the questions or follow the directions provided.

A. [1]Societies go through several stages in the production of goods. [2]In many less developed countries, most people produce their own products and then consume them. [3]As a society continues to grow, however, a person's or household's special talents are recognized. [4]For example, one person may be very good at carpentry, one at baking bread, and one at growing vegetables. [5]Soon an exchange process takes place: "I'll trade you my bread or several loaves of it for the table and chair you've just built. [6]Chances are, I can bake the bread better and faster than you can, and I know you can build the tables and chairs better than I." [7]Eventually, several households begin to produce surplus products beyond their immediate needs. [8]People produce more and more until they no longer have time to engage in exchange activity. [9]They then turn their products over to one person or to a store that agrees to handle all further exchange activities. [10]In this manner, a modern marketing system is created.

1. The main pattern of organization for the above selection is
   A. list of items.
   B. time order.

2. A transition that introduces one of the major details of the paragraph is _____

   _____.

B. [1]From observing chimps in the wild, Jane Goodall made two important discoveries that brought her international fame. [2]One discovery was that chimps make and use tools. [3]As Goodall looked on, for instance, several chimps plucked long blades of grass, stripped off the leaves, licked one end to make it sticky, and poked the stem into a termite nest, pulling it out covered with termites. [4]These they licked off as a child would a lollipop.

   [5]In addition, Goodall discovered that chimpanzees eat meat—on a regular basis. [6]Goodall frequently saw them catch, kill, and devour bushbucks and bushpigs. [7]She also saw them frequently kill and eat monkeys and young baboons. [8]Indeed, Goodall saw her chimps throw rocks and use sticks as clubbing weapons.

3. The main pattern of organization for the above selection is
   A. list of items.
   B. time order.

4. The words that introduce the major supporting details of the passage are
   A. *as, for instance, indeed.*
   B. *one, in addition.*
   C. *frequently, also.*

(Continues on next page)

5–6. Complete the outline of the passage.

Main idea: Jane Goodall made two important discoveries about chimps.

Major supporting details:

1. _____

2. _____

C. (7–10.) Complete the map of the following textbook passage.

¹In some ways, the American criminal-justice system is like a "wedding cake" with four layers, representing different kinds of cases. ²In the top layer are notorious criminal cases that get heavy news coverage. ³Our image of the justice system—of elaborate trials, highly paid defense lawyers, endless appeals—is formed by these cases, but they are only a small fraction of the total. ⁴The second layer down is made up of other serious felonies—murders, rapes, robberies—that don't get as much news coverage. ⁵Most of these cases are "plea-bargained," but usually result in prison terms. ⁶In the next layer are "less serious" felonies, such as car theft, that may not result in prison terms. ⁷Finally, the lowest and largest layer is made up of the huge number of misdemeanors such as traffic violations. ⁸These cases are handled in a routine way, and they seldom result in jail terms.

The American Criminal-Justice System

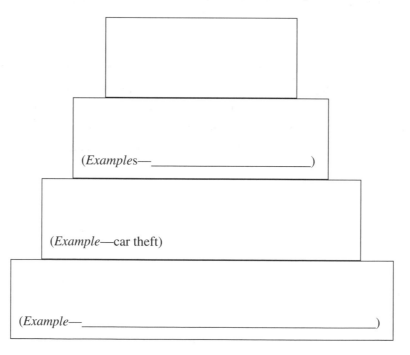

(Examples—_____)

(Example—car theft)

(Example—_____)

RELATIONSHIPS I: Test D

Read each textbook passage and answer the questions or follow the directions provided.

A. [1]In surveys of what people think about advertising, one of the most common and consistent complaints is that it is annoying to see the same old stuff over and over again. [2]Yet even though repetitive advertising is regarded as irritating, there are a couple of reasons why advertisers continue to use it. [3]First of all, repeated ads are cost-efficient. [4]With the high cost of creating and producing new advertising ideas and slogans, it makes sense to stick with proven winners. [5]Moreover, the familiarity brought about by repeated exposure to advertising has been found to create attraction and liking. [6]How familiarity can result in sales can be seen in a typical trip to the grocery store in search of a laundry detergent. [7]We go to the detergent section and see a staggering array of brand names. [8]Because it doesn't much matter which one is purchased, we may simply reach for the most familiar one—and chances are it is familiar because we've heard and seen the name on television commercials over and over again. [9]Research studies have confirmed that more exposure results in increased liking.

1. The main pattern of organization of the selection is
   A. list of items.
   B. time order.

2. The major supporting details of the paragraph are introduced with the transitions *first of all* and _____.

B. [1]According to most social psychologists, stereotypes are basically false for three reasons. [2]First of all, they exaggerate the differences between groups (for example, Irishmen are drunks; Jews don't drink), and they take no account of the millions of individual differences within groups. [3]Furthermore, they often carry the totally unproven assumption that the group's behavior is biologically determined. [4]Third, many of the traits assigned through stereotyping are simply not there. [5]For example, contrary to popular opinion, homosexuals do not have a distinct personality type. [6]According to research, most homosexuals are indistinguishable from heterosexuals in personality as well as in manner and appearance. [7]Also, women are not the bad drivers many believe they are. [8]Every year the percentage of women drivers responsible for automobile accidents is much smaller than the percentage of male drivers causing accidents.

3. The main pattern of organization of the selection is
   A. list of items.
   B. time order.

4. The topic sentence is sentence number _____.

5. The major supporting details are signaled with the transitions *first of all,*

_____, and *third.*   *(Continues on next page)*

6. The minor supporting details are
   A. steps.
   B. events.
   C. examples.

C. ¹Failure to cope adequately with organizational stress may lead to burnout. ²The burnout process occurs gradually. ³In fact, experts describe five stages of burnout. ⁴Stage one is the honeymoon. ⁵Beginning a new career is an exciting challenge. ⁶Learning to adapt to your new environment absorbs an enormous amount of valuable energy, but during this period you also must learn to adapt to stress. ⁷If you fail to do so, then you may move to the second stage. ⁸For many people, stage two begins with a vague realization that the honeymoon is over. ⁹Enthusiasm for the job begins to fade, and job dissatisfaction, inefficiency, fatigue, sleep disturbances, and escape activities may begin to bother you. ¹⁰Stage three of job burnout is marked by physical and psychological symptoms: chronic exhaustion, physical illness, anger and depression. ¹¹This may be when you first realize that you are in trouble. ¹²By stage four, symptoms become critical. ¹³Pessimism and frustration take over, and as a victim of burnout, you are obsessed with escaping. ¹⁴Finally, for the victim of professional burnout, stage five probably means that alcoholism, drug abuse, or heart disease have emerged as serious problems.

7. The main pattern of organization for the above selection is
   A. list of items.
   B. time order.

8–10. Complete the map of the paragraph by finishing the main idea and filling in the missing major details.

   Main idea: According to experts, the burnout that results from organizational stress takes place in _____.

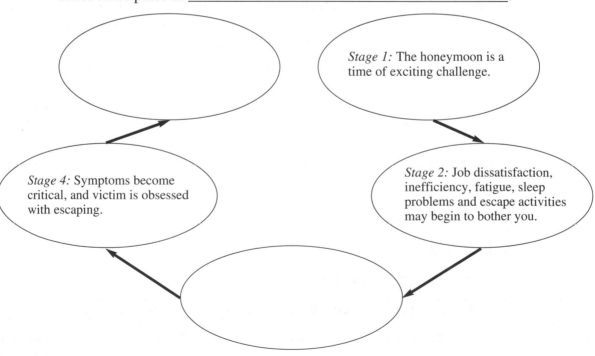

Stage 1: The honeymoon is a time of exciting challenge.

Stage 4: Symptoms become critical, and victim is obsessed with escaping.

Stage 2: Job dissatisfaction, inefficiency, fatigue, sleep problems and escape activities may begin to bother you.

RELATIONSHIPS II: Test A

A. Fill in each blank with an appropriate transition from the box. Use each transition once.

despite	for example	however
reason	similar	

1. ¹Plants can be surprisingly destructive. ²Invading plants, _____, can relatively quickly turn an abandoned factory site into a field and then into woodland. ³Dense vegetation completely overwhelms abandoned cities, especially in tropical areas, and the cities can be lost for centuries.

2. ¹Today, beach towns are popular tourist resorts. ²_____, until a couple of hundred years ago, the seacoast was a place of danger. ³People stayed away from the coast because they feared capture by pirates or slave-raiders. ⁴In fact, many of the places we might like to go to in order to "get away" on vacation were once feared and avoided. ⁵Have you ever daydreamed of being stranded on a tropical island? ⁶That was once no daydream, but a terrible punishment for sailors found guilty of mutiny.

3. ¹Clothing is not only a means of keeping warm and decently covered; it's also a means of communication. ²We affect others' perceptions of us by the way we dress. ³If we are trying to establish ourselves as part of a group, we adopt the dress style of that group. ⁴That's the _____ an applicant for an executive position shows up for the interview dressed like an executive: dark suit, conservative shoes, subdued jewelry.

4. ¹In the early days of industrialized America, many children worked full-time in factories and even mines. ²_____ their small size and youth, children would often work up to fourteen hours a day. ³Work conditions were often brutal, with children subjected to such horrors as being chained to their beds at night and to their factory machines during the day.

5. ¹Try the following experiment. ²Ask a friend to drop a large handful of loose papers in the middle of a busy sidewalk, pretending that it is an accident. ³Observe from afar how many people stop to help your friend pick up the papers. ⁴Then try the same thing a second time, using the same or a _____ location at a similarly busy hour. ⁵This time, however, you should help pick up the papers, all the while pretending to be a stranger. ⁶You will probably find that when you help, others are more likely to help, too.

(Continues on next page)

B. Label each item with the letter of its main pattern of organization.

A Definition and example
B Comparison and/or contrast
C Cause and effect

_____ 6. [1]Artificial intelligence (AI) is a term that describes computer programs that solve problems by "thinking" the way people do. [2]Most of these programs are based on sets of rules similar to logical thinking. [3]One AI program, for instance, was designed to diagnose infectious diseases. [4]It is about as efficient as most doctors. [5]In some fields, such as geology, AI programs have solved problems far more quickly than people could.

_____ 7. [1]The high cost of college today causes problems for many students in more ways than one. [2]For one thing, it undoubtedly prevents some students from attending college in the first place. [3]Also, high tuitions affect the amount of time available for studying; because loans and scholarships are hard to get, many students have to put in numerous hours at work in order to afford school. [4]Finally, those who do manage to get loans know that they must begin their careers with large debts.

_____ 8. [1]Back in 1800, American farmers worked 56 hours for every acre of wheat they raised. [2]In return, they harvested an average of 15 bushels for each hard-worked acre. [3]Today American farmers farm their wheat fields while riding in the air-conditioned cabs of huge diesel tractors and self-propelled combines. [4]It takes them an average of 2.8 hours a year to farm an acre of wheat. [5]And they average 31.4 bushels from each acre: twice as much wheat in 5 percent as many hours of work.

_____ 9. [1]An eidetic memory is the ability to recall every detail of a memory as clearly as if one were looking at a photograph. [2]An interesting example is the law student with eidetic memory who was accused of cheating on an examination because his test paper contained exactly the words in his textbook. [3]To prove his innocence, he studied an unfamiliar passage for five minutes and then wrote down more than four hundred words from it without making a mistake.

_____ 10. [1]When rangeland is overgrazed, the natural vegetation is destroyed and undesirable species take over. [2]If cattle herds graze on rangeland, they trample young plants, preventing their growth. [3]They also compact soil so that seeds cannot sprout. [4]This results in a reversion to an earlier stage of development, in which colonizing plants (usually undesirable) enter an area. [5]In addition, overgrazing accelerates erosion as topsoils are washed away, along with minerals and other nutrients.

RELATIONSHIPS II: Test B

Read each paragraph and answer the questions that follow.

A.   [1]If you can't get rid of a cold, the flu, or a nagging sore throat, the reason may be your toothbrush. [2]Studies at the University of Oklahoma Dental School have shown that your old toothbrush may carry the germs that are causing your illness. [3]The studies have found that people who change their toothbrushes about every two weeks recover from common winter ills faster than people who use their toothbrushes for a month or more. [4]Old toothbrushes can culture the germs that can cause colds, influenza, pneumonia, strep throat, diarrhea, and sinus disease. [5]Another study found that disease germs can live in an unused toothbrush for as long as a week. [6]They can start to thrive again every time you brush your teeth.

___ 1. The main pattern of organization of the selection is
   A. definition and example.
   B. cause and effect.
   C. comparison and/or contrast.

2. One transition that signals the pattern of organization is _____.

B.   [1]Identical twins such as Jack Yufe and Oskar Stohr share the same genes. [2]They were separated at six months of age, when their parents divorced. [3]Yufe was raised as a Jew, joined an Israeli kibbutz in his youth, and served in the Israeli navy. [4]Stohr was brought up as a Catholic and later became involved in the Hitler youth movement. [5]Despite the differences in their backgrounds, when they first met at the airport, both sported mustaches and two-pocket shirts and epaulets, and each carried a pair of wire-rimmed glasses with him. [6]Both read magazines from back to front. [7]Both excel at sports and have difficulty with math. [8]And both have similar personality profiles as measured by the Minnesota Multiphasic Personality Inventory.

___ 3. The main pattern of organization of the selection is
   A. definition and example.
   B. cause and effect.
   C. comparison and/or contrast.

4. One transition that signals the pattern of organization is _____.

(Continues on next page)

C. [1]"Regulators" are the subtle signals we use to control the give and take of conversation. [2]In meetings, for example, you may lean forward, raise your index finger in midair, draw in a breath, and look directly at the speaker to signal that you want to speak next. [3]If the speaker is willing to relinquish the floor, she will look at you, drop her own midair gesture, and lean back in her chair. [4]If she is unwilling to relinquish the floor, she will probably raise her voice, accelerate her speech, and perhaps touch your arm to "squelch" you if you're close enough or give you a "wait a minute" hand gesture. [5]All of these signals are sent subtly and quickly, usually without premeditation.

_____ 5. The main pattern of organization of the selection is
   A. definition and example.
   B. cause and effect.
   C. comparison and/or contrast.

6. The transition that signals the pattern of organization is _____.

D. [1]Female employment and small families make divorce more likely in modern societies. [2]A major result of the massive entry of women into the labor force has been to decrease the dependence of wives on their husbands for economic support. [3]This change has had beneficial effects. [4]For instance, woman need no longer cling to a brutal or drunken husband merely because she has nowhere else to turn. [5]But it also encourages some women to give up on a relationship more quickly. [6]Also, husbands have greater economic freedom to divorce wives who work because working wives are seldom granted a great deal of alimony.

_____ 7. The main pattern of organization of the selection is
   A. definition and example.
   B. cause and effect.
   C. comparison and/or contrast.

8. One transition that signals the pattern of organization is _____.

E. [1]In Third World cities, poverty and affluence exist side by side. [2]Skyscrapers tower over slums, and shantytowns spring up next door to luxurious apartment blocks and villas, continental restaurants, and nightclubs. [3]In most Third World cities, a small middle and upper class lives in an affluent style familiar to their American and European counterparts. [4]They own color televisions and VCRs, send their children to private schools, wear Italian suits and French fashions, and drive Japanese or German cars. [5]Indeed, they have privileges beyond the reach of most middle-class Americans, such as full-time, live-in household help (which they can afford because of the large numbers of unemployed). [6]At the opposite extreme are the great majority of urban residents. [7]They live in quite different conditions most Americans cannot imagine—not only without electricity, but without solid buildings, streets, sewers, toilets, or even running water.

_____ 9. The main pattern of organization of the selection is
   A. definition and example.
   B. cause and effect.
   C. comparison and/or contrast.

10. One transition that signals the pattern of organization is _____.

RELATIONSHIPS II: Test C

Read each paragraph and answer the questions that follow.

A. [1]A psychology professor introduced the same male guest lecturer to two different classes. [2]The first class was told to expect a rather cold, dull, uninteresting person. [3]The second class was told to expect a warm, intelligent, friendly lecturer. [4]The lecturer presented identical information in the same manner to both groups. [5]The first group found his lecture boring and did not ask questions; the second group found him warm and stimulating and asked many questions. [6]This experiment has been replicated successfully many times. [7]The outcome of these experiments suggests that telling someone what to perceive in another person will influence what is experienced.

____ 1. The main idea of the paragraph is expressed in
  A. sentence 1.
  B. sentence 4.
  C. sentence 7.

____ 2. The two patterns of organization of the selection are comparison-contrast and
  A. definition and example.
  B. cause and effect.

B. [1]In selective perception, we tend to see, hear and believe only what we want to see, hear, and believe. [2]As the late Canadian philosopher Marshall McLuhan pointed out, "Everyone has his own set of goggles," and we all think that what we see with our set of goggles is what everyone else sees. [3]Many studies have demonstrated selective perception at work. [4]One involved showing people an editorial cartoon from a Northern newspaper ridiculing the Ku Klux Klan; the cartoon was repeatedly interpreted as pro-Klan when shown to Southern Klan sympathizers. [5]A classic example of selective perception appeared in the early 1970s when television producer Norman Lear introduced the bigot Archie Bunker to American television audiences in the situation comedy *All in the Family.* [6]Bunker's prejudices were reflected in a number of controversial topics, such as sex, religion, and racism. [7]The character of Archie Bunker was designed to satirize American bigotry. [8]But what developed were Archie Bunker fan clubs and Archie Bunker T-shirts proclaiming America's number-one television bigot a folk hero. [9]Many people thought what he said was true and thus failed to get the message or see the satire.

____ 3. Which statement best expresses the main idea of the selection?
  A. Selective perception is the tendency to see, hear and believe only what we want to see, hear, and believe.
  B. The character of Archie Bunker was designed to satirize American bigotry.
  C. Bigots tend to interpret satire of prejudice as praise for bigotry.

____ 4. The paragraph mainly
  A. defines and illustrates "selective perception."
  B. explains the effects of bigotry.
  C. compares bigots with nonbigots.

(Continues on next page)

____ 5. The supporting details of the paragraph are
   A. reasons.
   B. contrasts.
   C. examples.

C. ¹Sociologists have identified several common reasons why people join cults. ²Many cult members come from homes filled with conflict; seeking to escape that conflict, they are drawn to the apparent security and acceptance offered by the cult. ³Another reason people join a cult is that they may be overwhelmed by the demands of adult life. ⁴The cult, with its strict rules and rigid discipline, relieves them from many personal decisions. ⁵Finally, many cult members are highly idealistic persons—they are gratified by the feeling that by joining the cult, they are committing their lives to the establishment of a better world.

____ 6. The two patterns of organization of the paragraph are list of items and
   A. definition and example.
   B. cause and effect.
   C. comparison and/or contrast.

7–10. Complete the map of the paragraph.

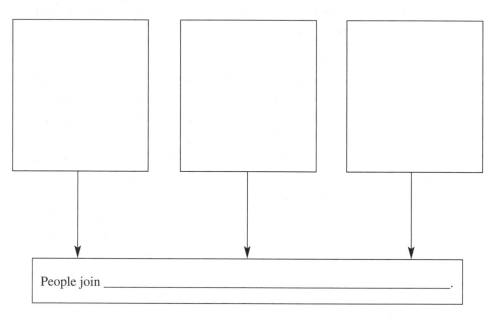

People join _____.

RELATIONSHIPS II: Test D

Read each paragraph and answer the questions or follow the directions provided.

A. [1]Unfortunately, 60 percent of all new businesses will not celebrate a sixth anniversary. [2]Why do some small businesses fail? [3]Although there is no set pattern, there are four common causes of failure. [4]First is managerial incompetence or inexperience. [5]Many businesses are started by people with little or no management training or experience. [6]Some people think that management is just "common sense." [7]But if managers do not know how to make basic business decisions, they are unlikely to be successful in the long run. [8]The second common cause of failure is neglect. [9]After the glamour and excitement of the grand opening, some entrepreneurs get discouraged and fail to focus on business as much as they should. [10]In short, starting a small business requires an overwhelming time commitment. [11]Small business owners who are unwilling to work long hours and perform many different functions are likely to fail. [12]A third common cause of failure is weak control systems. [13]A control system helps owners and managers monitor costs, production rates, productivity, and so forth. [14]If control systems do not signal approaching problems, managers may be in serious trouble before more visible difficulties alert them. [15]Finally, insufficient capital may contribute to failure. [16]Here is an oft-cited rule of thumb: A new business should have enough capital to operate at least six months without earning a profit. [17]Owners of new businesses are almost certain to fail if they expect to pay the second month's rent from the first month's profits.

_____ 1. The patterns of organization of the paragraph are list of items and
     A. definition and example.
     B. cause and effect.
     C. comparison and/or contrast.

2–4. Complete the outline of the paragraph by completing the main idea and filling in the two missing major details.

Main idea: There are four _____

_____

    1. Managerial incompetence or inexperience

    2. _____

    3. _____

    4. Insufficient capital

(Continues on next page)

B. [1]Cities in developing countries are noticeably different from those in wealthier nations. [2]Visitors often comment on the number of younger people in the less developed countries. [3]Almost half of all city residents in these countries are children and young people as compared to less than one quarter of the population of cities in developed countries. [4]Also, many unskilled workers found jobs in European and North American cities when the economies there became industrialized. [5]In contrast, one quarter of the work force is unemployed in a typical city in a developing country. [6]Although homeless people are found in Europe and North America, many more people live on the street and in improvised shacks in the less-developed nations. [7]In Mexico City, for instance, more than four million squatters live in improvised shelters.

5. The topic sentence of the selection is sentence number _____.

___ 6. The main pattern of organization of the selection is
   A. definition and example.
   B. cause and effect.
   C. comparison and/or contrast.

7–10. Complete the chart of the paragraph by filling in the missing heading and details.

	Cities in Wealthier Nations	_____ _____
Younger people	Less than one quarter of population	_____ _____
Employment	Jobs for many unskilled workers	_____ _____
_____	Some on the streets	Many more on the streets and in shacks

FACT AND OPINION: Test A

A. Five of the statements below are facts, and five are opinions. Identify statements of fact with an **F** and statements of opinion with an **O**.

_____ 1. The tarantula spider can live for as long as two years without food.

_____ 2. The first President to have been born in a hospital is Jimmy Carter.

_____ 3. The best-looking of all American Presidents was John F. Kennedy.

_____ 4. Cigarette advertising was banned on TV on January 1, 1971.

_____ 5. Congress should pass a law making cigarettes illegal.

_____ 6. Couples should know each other for at least a year before getting married.

_____ 7. For various reasons, some spouses take separate vacations.

_____ 8. In point of fact, it is always better for spouses to vacation together.

_____ 9. Boxing, an overly violent sport, should finally be outlawed.

_____ 10. Boxer James J. ("Gentleman Jim") Corbett never had a bloody nose or a black eye during his eighteen-year boxing career.

B. Here are short reviews taken from a newspaper movie guide. Some provide only factual reports; others contain opinions about the movie as well. Identify the factual reviews with an **F**; identify those that also contain the reviewer's opinion with an **F+O**.

_____ 11. **Panic Room, '02.** Jodie Foster, Forest Whitaker. A single woman and her daughter struggle to stay alive after three thieves break into their New York brownstone.

_____ 12. **Chicken Run. '00.** Mel Gibson, Julia Sawalha. Facing imminent death while laying eggs at Tweedy's English farm, a group of chickens plan to escape their prisonlike coop. A clever, funny comedy suitable for all ages.

_____ 13. **North by Northwest. '59.** Cary Grant, Eva Marie Saint. A comedy-thriller, with bewildered ad-man Grant chased cross country by both spies and the police. One memorable scene after another, including now-legendary crop-dusting and Mount Rushmore sequences.

(Continues on next page)

_____ 14. **Absolute Power, '97.** Gene Hackman, Ed Harris, Clint Eastwood. This thriller about murder and deceit at the highest levels of government doesn't live up to its possibilities.

_____ 15. **The Count of Monte Cristo. '02.** Jim Caviezel, Guy Pearce. A French sailor, framed and sent to an island prison, escapes and seeks revenge on those who betrayed him.

C. (16–20.) The passage below contains five sentences. Each sentence is fact or opinion. In addition, one sentence expresses both a fact and an opinion. Identify facts with an **F**, opinions with an **O**, and the **one** statement of fact *and* opinion with an **F+O**.

[1]The TV series *The Little House on the Prairie* was based on a series of books by Laura Ingalls Wilder. [2]Wilder's nine books, beginning with *Little House in the Big Woods,* tell about the author's life as part of a pioneer family in the American West. [3]The books give the finest firsthand picture of pioneer life ever written for children. [4]Wilder, who did not begin writing the stories until she was almost 60, had a really amazing memory for the details of her childhood. [5]Every school and public library should own several copies of Wilder's books.

1. _____   2. _____   3. _____   4. _____   5. _____

FACT AND OPINION: Test B

A. Five of the statements below are fact, and five are opinion. In addition, two statements include both fact and opinion. Identify facts with an **F**, opinions with an **O**, and statements of fact *and* opinion with an **F+O**.

_____ 1. It isn't fair for the police to ticket a car only minutes after the parking meter runs out.

_____ 2. The first parking meters were installed in Oklahoma City, Oklahoma, in July of 1935.

_____ 3. The first words spoken by Thomas Edison into a phonograph, his invention, were "Mary had a little lamb."

_____ 4. The voting machine was a more important invention than the phonograph.

_____ 5. Edison was the world's greatest inventor.

_____ 6. Yuma, Arizona, is a wonderful place to live.

_____ 7. Yuma, on average, receives more sunshine than any other city in the country.

_____ 8. Archeology, a fascinating field of study, is concerned with people and cultures of the past.

_____ 9. Archeologists study historic cultures by analyzing their objects and buildings.

_____ 10. Most high-school graduates should work for a year before attending college.

_____ 11. Some insects can live for as long as a year after their heads are cut off.

_____ 12. Here's a disgusting fact: By the time the average person is 70, he or she will have shed about forty pounds of dead skin.

(Continues on next page)

B. (13–15.) The following paragraph contains three sentences. One is fact, one is opinion, and one sentence combines fact and opinion. Identify the fact with an **F**, the opinion with an **O**, and the statement of fact *and* opinion with an **F+O**.

[1]People who think of Alaska as an unattractive frozen wasteland are just plain wrong. [2]Alaska is a land of various wildlife, varying climates, and hundreds of forms of plant life. [3]In fact, the highest mountains in North America are in Alaska, where they have a starring role in some unforgettable scenery.

1. _____   2. _____   3. _____

C. Below are passages from Ann Landers' column and a textbook. Identify each of the listed excerpts from the passages as either fact (**F**) or the author's opinion (**O**).

From Ann Landers:

[1]Dear Loomis: I have long supported the use of marijuana for medicinal purposes. [2]It has indeed proven helpful to asthmatics, as well as cancer and glaucoma patients. [3]Marijuana can and should be made available to physicians for these purposes. [4]But legalize it? [5]No. [6]We do not need any more stoned, zonked-out people on our streets and highways or anywhere else, for that matter.

_____ 16. It has indeed proven helpful to asthmatics, as well as cancer and glaucoma patients.

_____ 17. We do not need any more stoned, zonked-out people on our streets and highways or anywhere else, for that matter.

Textbook passage:

[1]The person most responsible for the growth of the automobile industry was Henry Ford, a self-taught mechanic from Greenfield, Michigan. [2]Ford had two brilliant insights. [3]The first was, in his words, "Get the prices down to the buying power." [4]Through mass production, cars could be made cheaply enough to put them within reach of the ordinary citizen. [5]Ford's second insight was in grasping the importance of high wages in stimulating output (and selling more automobiles). [6]The assembly line simplified the laborer's task and increased the pace of work; at the same time it made each worker much more productive. [7]Consequently jobs in Ford's plants became boring. [8]To offset this monotonous work, in 1914 Ford established the five-dollar day, an increase of about two dollars over prevailing wages. [9]Ford's profits soared along with sales; since he owned the entire company, he became a billionaire.

[10]Unfortunately, Ford's defects also had great impact on workers. [11]He paid high wages but tyrannized his employees. [12]He hired spies to investigate the private lives of his help and gangsters to enforce plant discipline. [13]So close was the supervision in the factory that workers devised the "Ford whisper," a means of talking without moving the lips.

_____ 18. Ford had two brilliant insights.

_____ 19. To make up for this boredom, in 1914 Ford established the five-dollar day, an increase of about two dollars over prevailing wages.

_____ 20. So close was the supervision in the factory that workers devised the "Ford whisper," a means of talking without moving the lips.

FACT AND OPINION: Test C

A. Identify each of the following textbook excerpts as fact (**F**), the author's opinion (**O**), or a combination of fact *and* opinion (**F+O**).

_____ 1. Some human eyes are so sensitive that on a clear, black night they can spot a candle flame more than thirty miles away.

_____ 2. Studies have repeatedly shown that age is no barrier to the benefits of exercise.

_____ 3. No reform movement of any era was more significant than the drive to abolish slavery.

_____ 4. Vitamin supplements are probably the most misunderstood and misused substances in the realm of health.

_____ 5. One technique used by psychologists to uncover unconscious motives and conflicts is dream analysis.

_____ 6. Claustrophobia is the fear of being confined in small places.

_____ 7. Nobody should seriously consider increases in prison sentences for offenders with poor employment histories.

_____ 8. Hormones, chemical substances produced in the body, play a role in emotions.

_____ 9. The U.S. government's travel service once published a guide to haunted houses around the country, a clear waste of taxpayers' money.

_____ 10. President Woodrow Wilson pressed the button which lit up the Woolworth Building.

_____ 11. The Woolworth Building was a hauntingly beautiful structure.

_____ 12. Paul Revere is famous for his midnight ride to warn the colonists that the British were coming during the American Revolution, but he should be equally honored for his fine work as a silversmith.

B. Following are passages from a textbook and a reference book. Identify each listed excerpt from the passages as either fact (**F**), opinion (**O**), or fact *and* opinion (**F+O**). (Only one of the statements combines fact and opinion.)

[1]The Shaker religious communities were founded by Ann Lee, an Englishwoman who came to America in 1774. [2]"Mother Ann" believed that Christ would come to Earth again as a woman and that she was that woman. [3]With a handful of followers, she founded a community near Albany, New York. [4]The group grew rapidly. [5]After her

(Continues on next page)

death in 1784, her movement continued to expand. ⁶By the 1830s her followers had established about twenty successful communities.

⁷The Shakers practiced celibacy. ⁸Believing the Second Coming was at hand, they saw no reason to add to the human race. ⁹Each group lived in a Family House. ¹⁰The sexes were strictly separated. ¹¹Property was held in common but controlled by elders. ¹²Because the Shakers put so much stress upon equality and voluntary acceptance of rules, members did not feel oppressed by those rules.

¹³The Shaker religion was joyful and intense. ¹⁴Much group singing and dancing provided the members with emotional release from their tightly controlled lives. ¹⁵An industrious, skillful people, they made a special virtue of simplicity. ¹⁶Some of their furniture is among the most classically beautiful ever designed in America.

_____ 13. The Shaker religious communities were founded by Ann Lee, an Englishwoman who came to America in 1774.

_____ 14. "Mother Ann" believed that Christ would come to Earth again as a woman and that she was that woman.

_____ 15. Each group lived in a Family House.

_____ 16. Some of their furniture is among the most classically beautiful ever designed in America.

¹After four miscarriages, Lady Bird finally gave birth to two daughters, Lynda Bird and Luci Baines. ²Thus the entire family (including the dog, Little Beagle Johnson) had the initials L.B.J. ³With their parents constantly busy, Lynda and Luci were raised largely by hired help. ⁴As Luci commented candidly about her father, "Eventually, I learned to love him as a person, not as a father—because he seldom had time to be a father." ⁵Nevertheless, LBJ took great pride in his children, and in 1968 he announced, "I'm the luckiest man alive. ⁶Neither of my girls drinks or smokes or takes dope, and they both married fine men."

⁷During the White House years, Lady Bird established herself as the most influential First Lady in history, barring only Eleanor Roosevelt. ⁸Aboard her own "Lady Bird Special," she became her husband's most effective campaigner and helped win approval for "the Lady Bird Bill," a significant piece of highway beautification legislation that eliminated thousands of billboards and junk heaps.

_____ 17. After four miscarriages, Lady Bird finally gave birth to two daughters, Lynda Bird and Luci Baines.

_____ 18. Thus the entire family (including the dog, Little Beagle Johnson) had the initials L.B.J.

_____ 19. During the White House years, Lady Bird established herself as the most influential First Lady in history, barring only Eleanor Roosevelt.

_____ 20. Aboard her own "Lady Bird Special," she became her husband's most effective campaigner and helped win approval for "the Lady Bird Bill," a significant piece of highway beautification legislation that eliminated thousands of billboards and junk heaps.

FACT AND OPINION: Test D

A. Identify each of the following textbook excerpts as fact (**F**), the author's opinion (**O**), or a combination of fact *and* opinion (**F+O**). (Two statements combine fact and opinion.)

_____ 1. The seas contain very few animals as outwardly unattractive as the oyster.

_____ 2. The Social Security Act was passed during the Great Depression.

_____ 3. In truth, romantic workplace relationships are generally not worth the trouble.

_____ 4. In the mid-1800s, women made up 85 percent of the work force in textile mills, yet they were kept out of supervisory positions.

_____ 5. When farmers complained about receiving "impersonal" typewritten letters from Sears, Roebuck in the 1870s, the retail company hired secretaries to write their business letters by hand.

_____ 6. Andrew Johnson, who became President following the assassination of Abraham Lincoln, was often extreme in his language, inept in his handling of opponents, and incorrect in his analysis of Southern conditions.

_____ 7. W.E.B. Du Bois was born to free parents in Massachusetts and became the first black to receive a doctorate from Harvard.

_____ 8. The sad fact is that neither Democrats nor Republicans have anything very useful to say about crime control.

_____ 9. Some people feel that the legends of King Arthur and the Knights of the Round Table were based on the life of a Celtic commander named Arthur who lived in the sixth century.

_____ 10. *Walden* is Henry David Thoreau's moving and beautifully written account of the two years he lived alone on the shores of Walden Pond.

B. (11–15.) The passage below contains five sentences. Each sentence expresses a fact, the author's opinion, or a combination of fact and opinion. Identify each sentence as fact (**F**), opinion (**O**), or fact *and* opinion (**F+O**).

   [1]Red is the most common color for barns throughout the United States. [2]It's fortunate that red is such a good color for barns because the early farmers who established the tradition didn't have other paint colors to choose from. [3]Pioneer farmers painted their barns with a mixture of skim milk, linseed oil, lime, and iron oxide, with the iron oxide furnishing the red color to the mixture. [4]Since outdoor paints are now available in a variety of colors, today's farmers paint their barns red out

(Continues on next page)

of choice, not necessity. [5]Everyone of taste would certainly agree that the countryside would be less beautiful if it were dotted with, for example, jet-black, purple or ultramarine barns.

1. _____   2. _____   3. _____   4. _____   5. _____

C. Read the following passage from an article in *Fortune* magazine, and then identify each of the listed excerpts from the passage as fact (**F**), the author's opinion (**O**), or a combination of fact *and* opinion (**F+O**). (Only one of the excerpts combines fact and opinion.)

[1]There was plenty of gossip in the corridors of Levi Strauss when Donna Goya, a personnel manager and rising star, cut back to a three-day-a-week work schedule. [2]"One of my colleagues thanked me for taking myself out of the running," she recalls. [3]Two years later, with her son in kindergarten, Goya returned to regular hours—and a promotion to director of personnel. [4]The colleague who was glad to see her leave? [5]"Now he works for me."

[6]Donna Goya belongs to a pioneering group of managers and professionals who are breaking the stranglehold of the five-day workweek to devote more time to other aspects of their lives, such as caring for a young child or an elderly parent. [7]These men and women have told their companies that, for a while, they will require flexible work schedules. [8]The surprise is that, in many cases, their careers are prospering. [9]It's still an uphill battle against well-established corporate practice, but by now enough companies have tried this kind of new approach that some lessons can be learned. [10]And they ought to be.

[11]*Flexible* is a term that covers a variety of arrangements: hours other than nine to five, part-time work, job sharing, leaves of absence, working at home. [12]From the company's perspective, the theory goes, allowing employees to work fewer and more flexible hours is a powerful way to attract and retain top-caliber people. [13]Adaptable schedules should also promote a sense of empowerment among workers and a feeling that the company trusts them. [14]Most important, these work arrangements enable dual-career parents to address the serious societal issue of raising children responsibly.

[15]Sounds great. [16]Why is it, then, that employees even of seemingly progressive companies still encounter a lot of resistance when they try to take advantage of the option? . . .

[17]Now some of the most forward-looking corporations—among them American Express, IBM, Levi Strauss, NCNB, and PepsiCo—are systematically trying to promote flexibility throughout their organizations.

_____ 16. Two years later, with her son in kindergarten, Goya returned to regular hours—and a promotion to director of personnel.

_____ 17. These men and women have told their companies that, for a while, they will require flexible work schedules.

_____ 18. And they ought to be.

_____ 19. *Flexible* is a term that covers a variety of arrangements: hours other than nine to five, part-time work, job sharing, leaves of absence, working at home.

_____ 20. Now some of the most forward-looking corporations—among them American Express, IBM, Levi Strauss, NCNB, and PepsiCo—are systematically trying to promote flexibility throughout their organizations.

INFERENCES: Test A

A. After reading each selection below, write the letter of the best answer to each question.

[1]In colonial America, anyone could become a physician merely by adopting the label. [2]There were no medical schools or medical societies to license or regulate what was a free-for-all trade. [3]Sometimes clergymen tried to provide medical care to their parishioners, and care of a sort was offered by all kinds of laypeople as well. [4]Documents of the time record a doctor who sold "tea, sugar, olives, grapes, anchovies, raisins, and prunes" along with medicinals. [5]Documents also tell of a woman who "Acts here in the Double Capacity of a Doctoress and Coffee Woman." [6]Training for medical practice, such as it was, was given by apprenticeship.

___ 1. The passage suggests that in comparison to today, a medical practice in colonial America
   A. must have been harder to establish.
   B. probably required more study.
   c. was less likely to be full-time.

___ 2. Considering the medical training and care, we might conclude that in colonial America
   A. most doctors did medical research.
   B. people were lucky to get good medical care.
   c. very few people would have been considered qualified to be medical apprentices.

[1]CPR—or cardiopulmonary resuscitation—is a life-saving procedure that forces oxygen-rich blood through a body in which the heart has stopped. [2]A person is not "dead" until his or her brain has died, which happens after about six minutes once the heart has stopped pumping blood through the brain. [3]When a qualified person does CPR, he or she presses on the patient's chest, squeezing the stopped heart between the breast bone and the spine, which forces blood through the body. [4]Between each series of pumps, the rescuer breathes into the victim's mouth, sending fresh oxygen into his lungs and into the blood. [5]Many people are alive today because of CPR.

___ 3. After someone's heart has stopped,
   A. people on the scene should wait for medical personnel to do CPR.
   B. CPR must be performed within about six minutes.
   c. CPR must be performed at a hospital.

___ 4. Essentially, CPR duplicates some of the activity of the
   A. brain.
   B. spine.
   c. heart.

(Continues on next page)

_____ 5. Pumping blood through the body during CPR is not enough because

    A. the pumping involves pressing on the patient's chest.

    B. the blood needs to receive oxygen.

    C. the pumped blood eventually reaches the brain.

B. (6–10.) Below is the beginning of an essay titled "The Plot Against People" by *New York Times* columnist Russell Baker. After reading the passage, check the **five** statements which are most logically supported by the information given.

inanimate: lifeless   *idle:* not busy

classified: grouped   *cunning:* slyness

¹Inanimate objects are classified scientifically into three major categories—those that break down, those that get lost, and those that don't work.
²The goal of all inanimate objects is to resist man and ultimately to defeat him, and the three major classifications are based on the method each object uses to achieve its purpose. ³As a general rule, any object capable of breaking down at the moment when it is most needed will do so. ⁴The automobile is typical of this category.
⁵With the cunning peculiar to its breed, the automobile never breaks down while entering a filling station which has a large staff of idle mechanics. ⁶It waits until it reaches a downtown intersection in the middle of the rush hour, or until it is fully loaded with family and luggage on the Ohio Turnpike. ⁷Thus it creates maximum inconvenience, frustration, and irritability. . . .
⁸Many inanimate objects, of course, find it extremely difficult to break down. ⁹Pliers, for example, and gloves and keys are almost totally incapable of breaking down. ¹⁰Therefore, they have had to evolve a different technique for resisting man.
¹¹They get lost. ¹²Science has still not solved the mystery of how they do it, and no man has ever caught one of them in the act.

_____ 1. We can conclude that the author does not own an automobile anymore.

_____ 2. The author writes about "inanimate objects," but describes them as having some characteristics of living beings.

_____ 3. The author has probably had frustrating experiences with things that broke down, got lost, and didn't work.

_____ 4. The author assumes his readers have had frustrating experiences with things breaking down, getting lost, and not working.

_____ 5. The essay appears to be about all types of "inanimate objects," both manmade and objects found in nature.

_____ 6. The passage's humor partly stems from the author's exaggerations.

_____ 7. We can conclude from the essay that the author often writes about science.

_____ 8. The passage's humor partly stems from the truth behind the author's points.

_____ 9. When the author refers to science and scientific classification, he expects to be taken seriously.

_____ 10. In real life, the author tends to lose things more often than others do.

INFERENCES: Test B

A. Following is a poem by the American writer Stephen Crane (1871–1900). Read it, and then write the letters of the inferences which are most logically supported by the poem.

I Stood Upon a High Place

I stood upon a high place,
And saw, below, many devils
Running, leaping,
And carousing in sin.
One looked up, grinning,
And said, "Comrade! Brother!"

____ 1. In saying he "stood upon a high place," the speaker suggests that he felt
   A. more righteous than the devils he saw.
   B. jealous of the playful devils.
   C. beneath the devils he saw.

____ 2. In saying "Comrade! Brother!" the devil means to imply that
   A. the speaker is an angel.
   B. the speaker is friendly.
   C. the speaker is also a sinner.

B. After reading the passage below, write the letter of the best answer to each question.

   ¹One wintry night in 1890, about four hundred Indians set up camp near Wounded Knee Creek, South Dakota. ²When they awoke the next morning, they found themselves surrounded by U.S. soldiers. ³On the hilltop above were numerous machine guns. ⁴When the soldiers ordered the Indians to hand over any weapons they might have, the Indians refused. ⁵The soldiers began searching for weapons. ⁶Then someone fired a shot. ⁷Immediately, the machine guns started blasting—cutting down Indian men, women, and children. ⁸Within a short time, all were killed. ⁹Several days later, the frozen bodies were tossed into a common grave. ¹⁰Instead of condemning the soldiers, the government awarded the troop twenty-six Medals of Honor and labeled the event a "battle." ¹¹It was the last fought against the American Indian.

____ 3. The passage suggests that
   A. the first shot was fired by a U.S. soldier.
   B. the first shot was fired by an Indian man.
   C. historians don't know who fired the first shot.

____ 4. We can conclude that the author feels
   A. the U.S. soldiers deserved the Medals of Honor.
   B. the event was more of a massacre than a battle.
   C. the Indians were given a fair chance to avoid being shot down.

(Continues on next page)

C. (5–10.) After reading the passage below, check the **six** statements which are most logically supported by the information given.

   ¹Our heartbeat, sleeping habits, brain activity, body temperature, and much more operate in certain rhythms or cycles. ²Scientists called chronobiologists try to understand how our "internal clocks" operate to regulate such cycles. ³One experiment conducted by chronobiologists involved placing a twenty-seven-year-old woman in an underground cave for 130 days. ⁴She was cut off from any way to measure the passage of time—there was no natural light in the cave, nor any clocks. ⁵The temperature was a constant sixty-nine degrees. ⁶When the woman was brought out of the cave at the end of the four-month period, her sleep cycle had changed dramatically. ⁷She would stay awake twenty to twenty-five hours, then sleep about ten hours. ⁸Her menstrual cycle had stopped. ⁹She believed she had been in the cave for only two months.

_____ 1. Chronobiologists are apparently biologists who specialize in human rhythms and cycles.

_____ 2. The experiment suggests that the human "internal clock" is influenced by such external cues as light and temperature changes.

_____ 3. The woman in the experiment never returned to the condition she was in before the experiment.

_____ 4. The woman spent four months in total darkness.

_____ 5. In the absence of a clock or the natural light and darkness of a day, it can be hard to judge how much time has passed.

_____ 6. Experiments can reveal much about human behavior that is not otherwise readily apparent.

_____ 7. Some of the effects on the woman in the experiment probably resulted from having no exercise at all for 130 days.

_____ 8. The researchers probably considered sixty-nine degrees to be a pretty comfortable temperature for humans.

_____ 9. The rhythm of the human body is usually not influenced by the natural rhythm of a day on Earth.

_____ 10. The woman in the experiment probably planned for numerous activities to keep her busy and interested while she was in the cave.

INFERENCES: Test C

A. After reading the textbook selection, write the letter of the best answer to each question.

[1]A century ago, a federal statute known as the Comstock Law made it illegal to distribute birth-control information and materials through the mails. [2]Druggists who sold contraceptive devices were arrested. [3]Various states had their own legislation concerning contraception. [4]Some made it a crime to distribute contraceptive literature. [5]Others forbade physicians to prescribe contraceptive devices. [6]Some even (as in Connecticut) made it against the law for couples—single or married—to use contraceptive devices.

[7]Many of these anticontraceptive measures continued into the present century, some until recently. [8]The clergy denounced birth control as sinful. [9]Theodore Roosevelt warned of "race suicide." [10]Condoms were referred to as "rubber articles for immoral use." [11]In the 1920s, the birth-control-movement leader Margaret Sanger needed diaphragms to distribute to women who came to her birth-control clinic. [12]She was unable to obtain such contraceptives in the United States and had to purchase them from abroad. [13]American manufacturers were by then permitted to manufacture contraceptive devices. [14]But they refused to make the reliable Mensinga diaphragm and, instead, made unsatisfactory cervical caps. [15]However, it was illegal to import contraceptives. [16]Margaret Sanger's clinic therefore obtained them through illegal channels. [17]The diaphragms were imported from Germany by way of Canada and then smuggled across the border in oil drums.

_____ 1. Roosevelt's warning of "race suicide" suggests that some opponents of contraception believed
   A. unmarried people should have children.
   B. there was no reliable way to prevent conception.
   C. if contraception were allowed, a low birthrate might lead to extinction.

_____ 2. The passage clearly implies that in the 1920s,
   A. women were content to let men handle contraception.
   B. some women were willing to risk arrest in order to get good contraceptives.
   C. most women were not religious at all.

_____ 3. From the passage we can conclude that in the 1920s,
   A. men led the birth-control movement.
   B. American contraceptive manufacturers did not fully respond to the demands of the market.
   C. the Comstock Law was still valid.

_____ 4. We can conclude that
   A. in reality, American laws about birth control have changed very little since a century ago.
   B. throughout the twentieth century, religious leaders had the most influence on views about birth control.
   C. many Americans' views on birth control have changed since the Comstock Law.

(Continues on next page)

B. (5–10.) After reading the textbook passage below, check the **six** statements which are most logically supported by the information given.

¹Maria Lopez gets up early six days a week to open up the small *bodega* (store) she runs in Saucillo, a village in the state of Chihuahua in northern Mexico. ²Señora Lopez stocks a limited number of items for her customers. ³She sells some products that require refrigeration, such as milk, eggs, meats, and vegetables, as well as staples like flour, salt, sugar, and canned goods.

⁴Most of Maria's customers work in a nearby oil refinery or are farmers. ⁵To help feed their families, many grow some of their own food and raise animals. ⁶Maria calls nearly all her customers by their first names and always attends their christenings, weddings, and funerals. ⁷She saves the freshest produce and best cuts of meat for her favorite customers and even keeps up with their diets.

⁸Tony Lopez, Maria's third cousin, manages a large Kroger supermarket on the west side of San Antonio, Texas. . . . ⁹Tony tries to spend at least an hour a day on the shopping floor chatting with customers and employees. ¹⁰But most of his time is taken up meeting with route salespeople for various grocery distributors and checking with Kroger's regional buyers.

¹¹Keeping such a mammoth store fully stocked requires careful planning, buying, and coordinating. ¹²Each morning, a computer printout from Kroger's regional office in San Antonio tells Tony the previous day's sales. ¹³It also provides a great deal more information: how many quarts of milk, crates of grapefruit, boxes of Tide (in each size), and packages of Green Giant frozen peas were sold.

_____ 1. Although Maria Lopez and Tony Lopez get their information in different ways, both are well-informed about their customers' needs and tastes.

_____ 2. Like Maria, Tony probably calls most of his customers by their first names.

_____ 3. Maria Lopez is more a part of her customers' lives than Tony Lopez is of his.

_____ 4. Despite the differences in their stores, Maria and Tony probably earn very similar incomes.

_____ 5. We can assume that a smaller percentage of Tony's customers grow vegetables or raise animals than the percentage of Maria's customers who do.

_____ 6. A computerized analysis of stock would be as useful for Maria's work as it is to Tony's.

_____ 7. Unlike Tony's store, Maria's store is not part of a supermarket chain.

_____ 8. The differences between Maria's and Tony's stores are closely tied to the differences between the communities they serve.

_____ 9. Since Tony has a much larger and more modern store to work in, he must enjoy his work a lot more than Maria does.

_____ 10. The Kroger customers expect less of a personal relationship with their store's manager than the *bodega*'s customers do.

INFERENCES: Test D

A. (1–6.) Read the following textbook passage, and then check the **six** statements which are most logically supported by the information given.

[1]Some behavioral psychologists have suggested that the personality could be precisely molded by training. [2]However, research now indicates that a child's temperament is probably predetermined, at least to some extent. [3]That is not to say that parents cannot guide and advise their children and help them to achieve a sense of self-worth. [4]For instance, setting limits for an aggressive child or gently urging a shy one to try new experiences could help youngsters to realize their full potential. [5]But trying to force a child to fit a particular model would probably be counterproductive.

[6]One therapist advises against attempts to radically redesign the personality. [7]Rather, he quotes a rabbi to illustrate the wisdom of trying to develop what is uniquely oneself. [8]The rabbi said that when he reached the kingdom of God, he knew he would not be asked, "Why weren't you Moses? Why weren't you David?" but "Why weren't you fully yourself?"

_____ 1. The author feels that parental guidance is not important.

_____ 2. The passage suggests that with guidance, a very shy child can become at least a little more outgoing.

_____ 3. In the past, behavioral psychologists have believed that the personality could be significantly changed.

_____ 4. Personality is determined by a child's environment, not his genes.

_____ 5. Genetic makeup has a great deal to do with personality.

_____ 6. The author suggests that personality is determined only by genetic makeup.

_____ 7. The rabbi probably believed that everyone has a unique contribution to make to society.

_____ 8. The author would probably agree with the idea that anyone can be a great artist, politician, or religious leader.

_____ 9. The passage suggests that it's better not to judge yourself in comparison to others.

_____ 10. The passage suggests that it is wise to be accepting of your child's fundamental temperament and interests.

(Continues on next page)

B. (7–10.) Read the following passage from *The Language of Clothes* by writer and educator Alison Lurie, and then check the **four** statements which are most logically supported by the information given.

banal: dull or commonplace

[1]In the past, sexual modesty was often proposed as the purpose of dress. [2]The Bible tells us that this was the original reason for wearing clothes: Adam and Eve, once they realized that they were naked, "sewed fig leaves together, and made themselves aprons." [3]Historically, however, shame seems to have played very little part in the development of costume. [4]In ancient Egypt, Crete and Greece, the naked body was not considered immodest; slaves and athletes habitually went without clothing, while people of high rank wore garments that were cut and draped so as to show a good deal when in motion.

[5]Some modern writers believe that the deliberate concealment of certain parts of the body originated not as a way of discouraging sexual interest, but as a clever device for arousing it. [6]According to this view, clothes are the physical equivalent of remarks like "I've got a secret"; they are a tease, a come-on. [7]It is certainly true that parts of the human form considered sexually arousing are often covered in such a way as to exaggerate and draw attention to them. [8]People done up in shiny colored wrappings and bows affect us just as a birthday present does: we're curious, turned on; we want to undo the package. . . .

[9]Many visitors to nudist camps report that the sight of all that uncovered flesh brings fatigue and a sense of being slightly unwell. [10]Later, after one gets used to it as the ancients were, it seems merely banal.

_____ 1. All cultures have agreed on the purpose of dress.

_____ 2. The author obviously feels that people should not dress in sexually arousing ways.

_____ 3. In ancient Egypt, Crete, and Greece, people showed more of their bodies than most Americans do today.

_____ 4. The author feels that nudist camps should not be allowed.

_____ 5. In ancient Egypt, Crete, and Greece, athletes were slaves.

_____ 6. From the passage we can conclude that clothing must have been very expensive in ancient Egypt, Crete, and Greece.

_____ 7. In a society without clothing, the naked body is not particularly thrilling.

_____ 8. The passage suggests that nudity in nudist camps generally leads to loose sexual behavior.

_____ 9. We might conclude from the passage that a tight dress can be more sexy to some than a topless bathing suit.

_____ 10. Behavior we consider basic may not be basic to other cultures.

PURPOSE AND TONE: Test A

A. In the space provided, indicate whether the primary purpose of each sentence is to inform (**I**), to persuade (**P**), or to entertain (**E**).

_____ 1. If you spend a dollar every minute, it will take you about twenty centuries to spend a billion dollars.

_____ 2. By selling candy and other junk food in the lunchroom, public schools are teaching poor nutrition; such "lessons" should not be allowed.

_____ 3. I asked my boss for a raise, so he moved my office from the basement to the second floor.

_____ 4 People should not be allowed to have children until they take a parenting class.

_____ 5. Between 93 and 95 percent of all fertile married couples choose to have children.

_____ 6. Insanity is hereditary. You get it from your kids.

_____ 7. Have your eyes checked at the We Care Eye Care Center, where we sell glasses at a discount to families.

B. Each of the following passages illustrates one of the tones named in the box below. In each space provided, write the letter of the tone that applies to the passage. Two tone choices will be left over.

A. ironic	B. annoyed	C. enthusiastic
D. distressed	E. forgiving	

_____ 8. [1]Strawberries are now available in the markets, and what a winning crop! [2]In contrast to last year's berries, which were badly affected by poor weather conditions, these are plentiful, delicious, and relatively inexpensive. [3]They will make a fine climax to any meal, whether under a dollop of sour cream laced with brown sugar or crushed over a scoop of vanilla ice cream. [4]In fact, these luscious berries are so sweet, they can stand very well on their own. [5]Strawberry lovers won't be disappointed.

_____ 9. [1]I visited my grandmother in a nursing home yesterday. [2]Ninety-two years old and partially paralyzed by a stroke, she now struggles to feed herself and is irreversibly bound to her bed or wheelchair. [3]Once vital and fiercely independent, she is now frail and incapable of even using the bathroom unassisted. [4]Mortified by her dependence on others, her moods range from quiet acceptance to whining complaint. [5]I do not see evidence of a divine plan in this situation. [6]Maybe there is no divine plan; or perhaps I am just not wise enough to see it.

(Continues on next page)

_____ 10. [1]Eighth-grader Terry met his friend Ron in front of Ron's house on the first day of summer vacation. [2]Ron looked at Terry's broad grin and remarked sympathetically, "I can't help but notice that you look utterly miserable. [3]You can confide in me—what's the matter?"

[4]Still smiling, Terry sighed and replied, "Well, who wouldn't be bummed out, confronted as we are with weeks stretching in front of us and nothing to do but waste the most beautiful months of the year on unimportant pursuits like basketball, fishing, and bike riding."

[5]"Yeah," whined Ron, as the two ambled towards the nearby basketball court. [6]"And the most depressing thing of all is that we don't get to see our valued colleague, Mr. Petersham, in the principal's office all summer."

[7]"We must try to endure it with superior courage," Terry replied, and then he dashed onto the court for his first lay-up.

(_Note:_ Select the tone that describes the boys' conversation.)

PURPOSE AND TONE: Test B

A. Eight quotations in the story below are preceded by a blank space. Identify the tone of each italicized quotation by writing in the letter of one of these tones. (Two tone choices will be left over.)

A. calming	B. bewildered	C. praising
D. matter-of-fact	E. threatening	F. sorrowful
G. remorseful	H. critical	I. pessimistic
J. grateful		

Tryouts for *The Wizard of Oz* were held Wednesday afternoon. The first student read for the part of Dorothy, the little girl who is swept away, along with her dog Toto, to the land of Oz.

_____ 1. *"Toto!"* she read. *"Where are we? Everything looks so strange! I don't think we're in Kansas anymore!"*

_____ 2. *"Very nice!"* said the teacher. *"You sound as if you've acted before!"*

Another student stepped up to read the lines of the Wicked Witch of the West.

_____ 3. *"Just try to stay out of my way!"* the "witch" hissed at Dorothy. *"I'm going to get you, the ruby slippers, and your nasty little dog, too!"*

Next a student tried out for the part of the Tin Woodman, who wanted a heart more than anything.

_____ 4. *"I'm just an empty kettle,"* he said with a sob. *"I am a heart-less piece of metal."*

While some students were reading for parts, others stood in the back of the room, whispering among themselves.

_____ 5. *"That last guy who read for the Cowardly Lion was really terrible,"* said one student.

_____ 6. *"I thought I'd try out for the part of Dorothy,"* a girl said, *"but I probably wouldn't have a chance. I never win anything."*

After all the students who wanted to read had their chance, the drama teacher spoke to them once more before they left the room.

_____ 7. *"Thank you all for coming. I really appreciate your interest in the drama department activities,"* she said with a warm smile.

_____ 8. As they began to leave, she added, *"My choices for the parts will be posted on the bulletin boards Friday morning."*

(Continues on next page)

B. In the space provided, indicate whether the primary purpose of each passage is to inform (**I**), to persuade (**P**), or to entertain (**E**).

_____ 9. [1]Until recently, it was commonly believed by intelligence experts that people reach the height of their intellectual peak by the time they're twenty. [2]Lately, however, scientists have discovered that our minds continue to grow long after we are fully developed physically. [3]In addition, some psychologists are expanding their notion of what makes up intelligence. [4]Dr. Robert Sternberg of Yale University, for example, outlines seven different areas of intelligence, including musical ability and self-knowledge.

_____ 10. [1]Cats are allowed to roam just about wherever they please (try and stop them), and even dogs have the run of the house, or at least of a portion of the house. [2]But pet birds are generally limited for most of their lives to the space defined by the four sides of a small cage. [3]Yet birds are born to flap and swoop through wide spaces of sky, unlimited neither by walls nor ceilings. [4]To keep a creature born with wings in a small space, unable to use its major natural means of transportation, is unfair. [5]People who want birds as pets should at least find ways to allow the birds to fly freely within one or two rooms of the house.

Name _____

Section _____ Date _____

SCORE: (Number correct) × 12.5 = _____%

PURPOSE AND TONE: Test C

Read each of the paragraphs below. Then carefully consider the questions that follow and write the letters of the best responses.

A. ¹Single, divorced, or widowed adults usually live either alone or with other family members. ²The idea of two unmarried adults joining forces in one household is one that has been too little explored in our society. ³When two divorced mothers and their children live together, everyone benefits. ⁴The adults can offer each other emotional support and practical assistance that isn't available in a single-parent household. ⁵The arrangement has similar advantages for unmarried or widowed persons. ⁶They can share expenses and household tasks while providing companionship for one another. ⁷Our commission should encourage such relationships by setting up a clearing house in which people can seek housing partnerships.

____ 1. The primary purpose of this paragraph is to
  A. inform.
  B. persuade.
  C. entertain.

____ 2. The tone of this paragraph is
  A. disappointed and hurt.
  B. disbelieving and uncertain.
  C. straightforward and caring.
  D. pessimistic and pleading.

B. ¹I can't thank Rob and Elsie sincerely enough for introducing me to Sheila. ²They promised me she was exactly my type, and how accurate they were—I've been yearning for a vain, shallow woman with the IQ of a turnip. ³Sheila and I hit it off immediately. ⁴When I picked her up in my Ford Escort, she wrinkled her adorable nose with exasperation and said, "I thought Elsie said you had a decent car." ⁵I took her to eat at Luigi's and was thrilled by the way she sneered and said, "You are a cheapskate, aren't you?" ⁶When I suggested we see a foreign film and she announced that she never sees anything with subtitles because she hates to read, I wanted to marry her on the spot. ⁷I'll certainly have to think of some way to repay my dear friends for fixing me up with such a marvelous girl.

____ 3. The purpose of this paragraph is to
  A. explain that the date with Sheila was a mistake.
  B. argue against blind dates.
  C. both of the above.

____ 4. The tone of this paragraph is
  A. uncertain but grateful.
  B. angry and bewildered.
  C. understanding and forgiving.
  D. ironic and mocking.

(Continues on next page)

C. [1]Many adult Americans, particularly males, do not have especially close friends. [2]This is unfortunate for a number of reasons. [3]The lack of close friends places an unrealistic burden on a person's spouse. [4]He or she is expected to provide all the other's emotional needs. [5]In addition, without close friends, adults become emotionally limited. [6]They lose the ability to express themselves freely to other people. [7]The Bangwa tribe of Western Africa, by contrast, value friendship so highly that parents assign each of their children a "best friend" in infancy. [8]Friends spend a great deal of time together throughout their lives. [9]The worst part of being old, complained one elderly Bangwa man, was that he had no best friend left to gossip with.

___ 5. The primary purpose of this paragraph is to
   A. present facts about adult friendship.
   B. argue that adult friendship is valuable.
   C. entertain with amusing customs of other cultures.

___ 6. The tone of the paragraph is
   A. excited.
   B. straightforward.
   C. fearful.
   D. disbelieving.

D. [1]"Secret Medical Breakthrough!" screams the headline. [2]"Melt Pounds Away While You Sleep!" [3]Then there's "The Cure For AIDS Is Right In Your Refrigerator!" [4]Or how about "Swiss Scientists Promise: You'll Never Have Another Cold!" [5]Advertisements and "news" stories like these appear in every supermarket tabloid and in the back pages of innumerable other publications. [6]They all seem based on the same doubtful premise: "Doctors don't want you to know the truth, but we're going to tell you anyway." [7]Don't let tabloid headlines tempt you into spending your hard-earned money. [8]The gullible readers who swallow these claims never seem to stop and ask why, if these stories of amazing cures and sure-fire remedies are true, they haven't made headlines in newspapers and other publications. [9]An AIDS cure? [10]A genuine weight-loss plan that involves no dieting or exercising? [11]If such stories were true, you wouldn't be reading about them first in the supermarket checkout aisle. [12]If the public stopped supporting these publications, they would no longer be able to falsely raise hopes for thousands of readers.

___ 7. The primary purpose of this paragraph is to
   A. explain the difference between tabloids and other newspapers.
   B. persuade readers not to support tabloids.
   C. tell amusing facts about tabloids.

___ 8. The overall tone of the paragraph is
   A. critical.
   B. uncertain.
   C. depressed.
   D. lighthearted.

PURPOSE AND TONE: Test D

Read each of the paragraphs below. Then carefully consider the questions that follow and write the letters of the best responses.

A. [1]Consumers may be influenced to buy an item not only by its price and quality, but also by the image it projects—and the image may be just that, only an image. [2]For instance, consider the cases of Haågen-Dazs ice cream and its competitor, Frusen Glådje. [3]Both are rich, so-called gourmet ice creams, and both cost considerably more than most other supermarket brands. [4]Both appeal to the consumer through their Scandinavian-sounding names, which imply that they are imported and thus superior or special in some way. [5]The Haågen-Dazs package even shows a map of Norway and Denmark, further suggesting a Scandinavian connection. [6]But that special "imported" quality is wholly in the mind of the consumer: Haågen-Dazs is manufactured in New Jersey, and Frusen Glådje in Philadelphia.

___ 1. The primary purpose of this paragraph is to
    A. inform.
    B. persuade.
    C. entertain.

___ 2. The tone of the paragraph can be described as
    A. mainly matter-of-fact.
    B. largely optimistic.
    C. greatly amused.
    D. very angry.

B. [1]Our world is paying a stiff price for chronic air pollution. [2]If dramatic changes are not made, pollutants will continue to rob us of money and health. [3]They damage buildings and automobiles. [4]Crops, livestock, roads, and metals are all hurt by air pollution. [5]We must pay millions to clean everything from soot-blackened buildings to curtains dirtied with pollutants. [6]If nothing else can persuade us to cut down on air pollution, perhaps the threats to our health will. [7]Our bodies are paying the highest price of all for living in a polluted land. [8]Breathing the air in New York City is equivalent to smoking several packs of cigarettes a day. [9]The poisons in the air accumulate in our bodies, leading to bronchitis, emphysema, and lung cancer.

___ 3. The primary purpose of this paragraph is to
    A. inform readers of facts about air pollution.
    B. persuade readers that air pollution must be reduced.
    C. amuse readers with details of ridiculous human error.

___ 4. The tone of this paragraph can be described as
    A. arrogantly sarcastic.
    B. sympathetic but angry.
    C. greatly concerned.
    D. bitterly revengeful.

(Continues on next page)

C. ¹I've been noticing a lot of cat-related items for sale recently: cat calendars, cat wallpaper, cat coffee mugs. ²These I cannot comprehend—cats are meant to be companions, not interior decorations. ³Worse are the cat psychology books, those with titles like *You Can Toilet Train Your Cat!* and *Command Your Cat to Sit, Stay, Lie Down!* ⁴First, I don't believe any of this is possible. ⁵I know when I suggest to my cat that he do anything other than lie in the sun, eat, and accept the adoration of humans, he gives me a cold stare that invites me to have my head examined. ⁶Second, I've always felt that much of a cat's charm lies in his refusal to cooperate with anyone's silly ideas about "training" him. ⁷If you want an animal to sit, stay, and lie down on command, get a German shepherd.

___ 5. The primary purpose of this paragraph is to
    A. seriously inform readers about cat-related products and books.
    B. persuade readers not to buy such products or books.
    C. entertain readers with observations about such products and books.

___ 6. The overall tone of this paragraph can be described as
    A. sarcastic and anxious.
    B. caring and forgiving.
    C. playful and humorous.
    D. regretful and surprised.

D. ¹You may think that buttons near the lower edge of jacket sleeves are just there for looks. ²That may be so today, but buttons on sleeves originally had a more practical purpose. ³During the frigid winter of 1882, Napoleon and his troops invaded Russia. ⁴As might be expected, many of his soldiers had runny noses from colds and flus, and—to put it delicately—they didn't have the neatest habits for dealing with this problem. ⁵This disturbed Napoleon, who was known to hate sloppiness and poor manners, so he instructed the military tailors to add metal buttons to the sleeves of his soldiers' jackets. ⁶Have you ever tried to wipe your nose on ice-cold buttons?

___ 7. The primary purpose of this paragraph is to
    A. inform readers about the unusual original purpose of buttons on sleeves.
    B. persuade readers to buy jackets with buttons on the sleeves.
    C. tell a joke.

___ 8. The tone of the paragraph can be described as
    A. ironic and humorous.
    B. loving and slightly sentimental.
    C. straightforward and somewhat amused.
    d. formal but passionate and outspoken.

ARGUMENT: Test A

A. (1–4.) In each group, one statement is the point of an argument, and the other statements are support for that point. Write the letter of the point of each group.

___ *Group 1*

    A. Curved streets discourage speeding cars.

    B. For residential neighborhoods, curved streets have advantages.

    C. The graceful lines of curved streets are more attractive than straight lines.

___ *Group 2*

    A. In stores, at bus stops, and at theaters, people are expected to wait for their turn in line.

    B. In cities, many everyday activities occur according to a system of rules.

    C. In North America, pedestrians keep to the right as a way to avoid running into others.

    D. Drivers are expected to stick to one side of the road.

___ *Group 3*

    A. In recent years, 62 percent of all traffic deaths took place at night.

    B. The chances of being in a fatal accident are nearly four times greater at night than during the day.

    C. Driving at night is less safe than in the daytime.

    D. Many dangerous corners and curves are poorly lit or unlit at night.

___ *Group 4*

    A. Dinosaur fossils teach us about animals that are now extinct.

    B. Fossils have "recorded" much about the past of the Earth and its inhabitants.

    C. Fossils of ferns found in the Arctic suggest climatic changes.

    D. Seashell fossils found high in the mountains indicate that those areas were once covered by salt water.

B. Each point is followed by three statements that provide relevant support and three that do not. In the spaces, write the letters of the **three** relevant statements of support.

Point: Selling cigarettes ought to be against the law.

    A. Cigarette smoking kills many more people than all illegal drugs combined.

    B. Today, tobacco growing is actually supported by government subsidies.

    C. Smoking makes clothing smell bad and stains teeth.

    D. Alcohol is another legal drug that kills numerous Americans every year.

    E. Nonsmokers are endangered by breathing the smoke from others' cigarettes.

    F. Tobacco is one of the most addictive of all drugs.

    5–7. *Items that logically support the point:* _____ _____ _____

(Continues on next page)

Point: Taking good care of a pet is healthy for the pet owner.

    A. Before-and-after studies have shown that petting an animal causes a decrease in many people's blood pressure.

    B. Owning a dog that needs a daily walk can encourage a senior citizen to get some much-needed exercise.

    C. Most people can easily afford the expense of pet food and veterinary care.

    D. In 1988, over 37 percent of American households owned at least one dog.

    E. The American Heart Association has said that pet owners are more likely to survive during the first year after a heart attack than people who don't own pets.

    F. In addition to cats and dogs, people have fish, birds, snakes, pigs, and even insects for pets.

8–10. *Items that logically support the point:* _____ _____ _____

ARGUMENT: Test B

A. Write the letter of the sentence that does **not** support the point of the argument in each paragraph.

> [1]Getting rid of the eyesores in a neighborhood does more than simply beautify; it can improve the economic and social life of an area. [2]Not long ago, a neighborhood in Philadelphia decided to improve its appearance by planting a community garden and installing trash cans. [3]As a result, neighbors spent more time together outdoors. [4]Thus graffiti writers and more serious offenders were discouraged from frequenting the area. [5]The cleaner streets and safer atmosphere also attracted more customers to local businesses. [6]Additional police on the streets also keep streets safer.

___ 1. Which sentence does not support the author's conclusion that getting rid of community eyesores can improve the local economic and social life?
   A. Sentence 3
   B. Sentence 4
   C. Sentence 5
   D. Sentence 6

> [1]Some people argue that music videos have hurt popular music by emphasizing looks rather than the music itself. [2]In fact, though, what music videos have done is bring new attention to another art form: dance. [3]Today, talented dancers can become top-name entertainers after being showcased by music videos. [4]Pop star Paula Abdul, for example, gained fame as a choreographer and dancer in music videos. [5]Ten or twenty years ago, dancers had far fewer opportunities to become known. [6]The music video industry has also created hundreds of new job opportunities for video producers, directors, and technicians. [7]Thanks to videos, dance is showcased in a way not seen since the days of song-and-dance musicals in the 1940s and 1950s.

___ 2. Which sentence does not support the author's conclusion that music videos have brought new attention to dance?
   A. Sentence 3
   B. Sentence 5
   C. Sentence 6
   D. Sentence 7

> [1]Be sure to include organic food in your supermarket basket. [2]First of all, eating organic produce may be good for you. [3]Nonorganic fruits, vegetables and grains are sprayed with pesticides; some of them, such as strawberries, are treated with a great deal of pesticides. [4]And some scientists believe that consuming pesticides over many years may turn out to cause cancer or other diseases. [5]In fact, some farmers are beginning to notice that they are getting sick themselves from using so many pesticides. [6]Also, organic food is becoming more and more popular. [7]Furthermore,

(Continues on next page)

organic farmers tend to build up and enrich the soil better than nonorganic farmers do. [8]Their methods are not only better for the Earth, they tend to produce better tasting fruits and vegetables.

___ 3. Which of the following sentences does not support the author's argument that it's a good idea to buy organic food?
- A. Sentence 2
- B. Sentence 6
- C. Sentence 7
- D. Sentence 8

B. For each group, read the three items of support (the evidence). Then write the letter of the point that is adequately supported by that evidence.

Group 1

Support:

- Janis Chavez served three terms on the city council.
- Ms. Chavez was head of the local planning commission for several years.
- She has also served as a special assistant to the mayor.

___ 4. Which of the following conclusions is best supported by the evidence above?
- A. Janis Chavez is the best qualified candidate for mayor.
- B. Janis Chavez has devoted her entire life to public service.
- C. Janis Chavez has always worked for the voters' best interests.
- D. Janis Chavez has broad experience in city government.

Group 2

Support:

- Stevie Wonder, a blind pianist, singer and composer, won several Grammy Awards, including one for his album "Songs in the Key of Life."
- Franklin Delano Roosevelt, the popular U.S. president who was elected for four terms, was paralyzed by polio.
- Beethoven, one of the greatest musical composers who ever lived, was completely deaf in his later years—even when he wrote and conducted his famous Ninth Symphony.

___ 5. Which of the following conclusions is best supported by the evidence above?
- A. Disabled people are more likely than others to achieve success in the field of music.
- B. Individuals with disabilities can achieve greatness.
- C. Disabled people become more famous than equally talented people who aren't disabled.
- D. People with disabilities aren't given enough opportunities to contribute to society.

ARGUMENT: Test C

A. Each of the two points below is followed by six items, three of which logically support the point and three of which do not. In the spaces provided, write the letters of the **three** items that logically support each point.

Point: Boxing should be banned.

 A. Promoters make a great deal of money.
 B. Boxers have died from injuries received in the ring.
 C. The sport of boxing began in ancient Greece.
 D. The main point of boxing is for opponents to badly hurt each other.
 E. Only a handful of boxers are very successful.
 F. Boxers have been permanently brain-damaged from the constant blows to the head.

1–3. *Items that logically support the point:* _____ _____ _____

Point: Sometimes the "newest thing" is something old that has made a comeback.

 A. Some cities that tore out their streetcar lines years ago are now putting them back.
 B. The basic black dress has never really gone out of fashion.
 C. Miniskirts, a 1960s fashion, became popular again in the 1980s.
 D. Fashions are more varied today than ever before.
 E. Many recent buildings have a 1930s look to them.
 F. The work of architect and designer Frank Lloyd Wright is still admired today.

4–6. *Items that logically support the point:* _____ _____ _____

B. Read the following three items of support (the evidence). Then write the letter of the point that is adequately supported by that evidence.

Support:

 • Many sports teams are named for Native American tribes or features of Indian cultures.
 • *Dances with Wolves*, a film sympathetic to Native Americans, was one of the hit movies of 1990.
 • The Indian peoples' reverence for nature has become a model for a new environmental ethic.

____ 7. Which of the following conclusions is best supported by the evidence above?
 A. Many cars have been named for Native American tribes
 B. Native Americans have fewer social problems than in previous times.
 C. Native Americans have influenced the general culture of the country.
 D. Native Americans are greater sports fans than other Americans.

(Continues on next page)

C. Read the paragraphs below, and then write the letter of the best answer to each question that follows.

[1]To have a successful budget, it is useful to include a category called "miscellaneous." [2]It is hard to remember every single item you buy. [3]And supermarket impulse purchases, such as gum and magazines, can result in a busted budget. [4]Certain supermarket purchases—such as candy—are best omitted from a health standpoint as well. [5]Extra gas for an unscheduled trip that requires spending beyond the usual fuel allowance can also ruin your spending plan. [6]You can even get in the red by buying ice cream cones at the dairy stand if they're not provided for under the food or entertainment categories. [7]Keeping track of these various expenses for several months will reveal an amount that is suitable to include under "miscellaneous."

___ 8. Which sentence is **not** relevant to the author's argument that a miscellaneous category can help you have a successful budget?
A. Sentence 3
B. Sentence 4
C. Sentence 5
D. Sentence 6

[1]The annual highway death rate has dropped 40 percent since the late 1970s primarily because of the safety features now available in vehicles. [2]Seat belts automatically present themselves, encouraging drivers and passengers to use them. [3]Air bags inflate instantly during impact, preventing deaths in many circumstances. [4]Anti-lock brakes often allow drivers to avoid an accident because the car can stop in a shorter distance with greater control. [5]Campaigns against drunk driving may also be making a dent in traffic accidents. [6]And fog lights improve visibility for the driver and make it easier for oncoming drivers to see the vehicle.

___ 9. Which statement is the point of the argument?
A. More safety features should be built into vehicles.
B. The safety features now available on vehicles are saving lives.
C. For too many years, automotive manufacturing companies resisted useful safety features.
D. One of the most important safety features on vehicles is the anti-lock brakes.

___10. Which statement is **not** relevant to the point of the argument?
A. Sentence 2
B. Sentence 3
C. Sentence 5
D. Sentence 6

ARGUMENT: Test D

A. The point below is followed by six items, three of which logically support the point and three of which do not. In the spaces provided, write the letters of the **three** items that logically support each point.

Point: Hypnosis can be a useful tool in various medical situations.
  A. Many medical professionals feel that hypnosis is nothing more than a form of entertainment.
  B. Hemophiliacs typically bleed so much from dental treatment that they need to be given several pints of blood, but some who were hypnotized during treatment needed no blood at all.
  C. People who are especially susceptible to hypnosis are often fantasy-prone.
  D. Suggestions given under hypnosis have improved headaches, asthma, and warts.
  E. Hypnosis has been found to be more effective than morphine in alleviating certain types of pain.
  F. People can be hypnotized to do something after they are brought out from a state of hypnosis.

  1–3. *Items that logically support the point:* _____ _____ _____

Point: The blood system is the distribution network of the body.
  A. The blood system carries food and oxygen to all the body's cells.
  B. The human body has about six quarts of blood.
  C. Circulating blood delivers hormones throughout the body.
  D. A decrease in the number of circulating red blood cells is called anemia.
  E. In an emergency, the liquid inside young coconuts can be used for blood transfusions.
  F. The blood system collects the body's wastes and brings them to the organs which remove them.

  4–6. *Items that logically support the point:* _____ _____ _____

B. Read the following three items of support (the evidence). Then write the letter of the point that is adequately supported by that evidence.

Support:
  • By 1860 (just before the Civil War began), one person out of every four in the U.S. lived in a city.
  • By 1890, one out of every three people in the U.S. lived in a city.
  • Half of all the people living in the U.S. in 1910 lived in a city.

____ 7. Which of the following conclusions is best supported by the evidence above?
  A. At the end of the 1800s and the beginning of the 1900s, there was a strong movement of people to the cities.

(Continues on next page)

B. In the years following the Civil War, people felt safer living in a city.

C. By the early part of the twentieth century, people no longer wished to settle in the West.

D. Since 1910, numerous people have gone back to rural America.

C. Read the paragraphs below, and then answer the questions that follow.

[1]Individual and family stress would be lessened and family togetherness increased if household responsibilities were assigned more evenly among family members. [2]Often wives who work full-time also do most of the work around the house, which makes their lives more stressful than necessary. [3]This stress often causes wives to resent their husbands and children, creating tensions throughout the family. [4]America's husbands have always been too self-centered. [5]A more fair distribution of household work would also free wives to spend more relaxing time together with their families. [6]If household work was more fairly divided, everyone's lives would undoubtedly be improved.

_____ 8. Which sentence is **not** relevant to the author's argument that assigning household responsibilities more evenly would lessen stress and increase togetherness?
   A. Sentence 2
   B. Sentence 3
   C. Sentence 4
   D. Sentence 5

[1]Forty-six out of ninety-three bottles of various brands of water tested in a major study had detectable levels of potentially harmful chemicals. [2]The levels didn't exceed Environmental Protection Agency limits—but, then, neither do those of tap water from urban areas with municipal water-treatment plants. [3]Indeed, it was found that most tap water can be as pure as—or purer than—some bottled waters. [4]And many taste just as good too. [5]It was also noted that tap water has as many "healthy" minerals as bottled water. [6]"The minerals in tap and bottled water are comparable, and vary only slightly," noted one dietician involved in the study. [7]Obviously, tap water can be as healthy or healthier than bottled water.

_____ 9. Which sentence expresses the point of the argument?
   A. Sentence 1
   B. Sentence 2
   C. Sentence 5
   D. Sentence 7

_____10. Which sentence is **not** relevant support for the point of the argument?
   A. Sentence 2
   B. Sentence 3
   C. Sentence 4
   D. Sentence 6

COMBINED SKILLS: Test A

After reading the passage, write the letter of the best answer to each question.

[1]The general public may still think of Girl Scouts as pigtailed lasses who earn merit badges for learning to apply tourniquets to stop bleeding. [2]However, that image is dated. [3]Girl Scouts today are more likely to be talking about making career choices or dealing with sexual pressure than about building campfires or knitting afghans.

[4]In recent years, the New York City-based Girl Scouts organization has been bombarded with criticism that its programs were no longer relevant to today's young females. [5]In response, Girl Scouts began overhauling the merit badge programs and updating its guidebooks for members. [6]Drugs, sex abuse, and teen pregnancy are all topics dealt with in Girl Scout books published since 1987. [7]Girls today can earn merit badges reflecting current issues [8]For example, badges are available for Girl Scouts who demonstrate their understanding of eating disorders such as anorexia and bulimia. [9]The result of these changes is that the Scouts organization helps members become more realistically prepared to deal with their lives.

____ 1. In sentence 5, the word *overhauling* means
   A. catching up with.
   B. improving.
   C. getting rid of.
   D. inventing.

____ 2. Today, Girl Scouts learn about such currently relevant issues as
   A. drugs.
   B. sexual abuse.
   C. eating disorders.
   D. all of the above.

____ 3. The relationship of sentence 8 to sentence 7 is one of
   A. contrast.
   B. time.
   C. illustration.
   D. comparison.

____ 4. The relationship between sentence 9 and the rest of the passage is one of
   A. illustration.
   B. comparison.
   C. cause and effect.
   D. contrast.

(Continues on next page)

_____ 5. The passage suggests that activities formerly associated with Girl Scouts include
  A. applying tourniquets.
  B. making career choices.
  C. understanding eating disorders.
  D. learning about teen pregnancy.

_____ 6. From the passage, one could conclude that
  A. Girl Scouts leaders were unconcerned by criticism of their organization.
  B. criticism of the Girl Scouts organization was unfair.
  C. most people preferred the old-style Girl Scouts organization.
  D. Girl Scouts leaders agreed that their organization needed updating.

_____ 7. Sentence 6 is a statement of
  A. fact.
  B. opinion.
  C. fact and opinion.

_____ 8. The author's main purpose is to
  A. inform.
  B. entertain.
  C. persuade.
  D. predict.

_____ 9. Which is the most appropriate title for this selection?
  A. Girl Scouts Changes: Too Little, Too Late
  B. Girl Scouts Change To Reflect Modern World
  C. The Girl Scouts Story
  D. Our Youth Learn About Social Problems

_____10. The main idea of this passage is that
  A. the Girl Scouts are an outdated organization.
  B. eating disorders are common problems among members of the Girl Scouts.
  C. the Girl Scouts have made changes to adapt to modern times.
  D. it is only recently that the Girl Scouts organization has truly served the needs of its members.

COMBINED SKILLS: Test B

After reading the textbook passage, write the letter of the best answer to each question.

[1]Many animals, including some insects, use visual clues to find their way. [2]For example, the female digger wasp lays eggs in a burrow in the soil. [3]She then flies off to capture her prey, which she stores in the burrow to feed her offspring when they hatch. [4]The famous animal-behavior scientist Niko Tinbergen studied the cues used by the female to relocate her burrow. [5]While the female was inside, Tinbergen surrounded the nest with pine cones. [6]When the wasp emerged, she flew around the nest before departing. [7]While she was gone, Tinbergen moved the cones about a foot away. [8]The returning wasp still sought her nest within the ring of cones. [9]Although the nest was in plain sight nearby, she was unable to locate it because the visual landmarks on which she relied had been shifted.

[10]Birds may also use landmarks, such as rivers and seashores, to find their way. [11]Several species migrate at night or over large expanses of ocean, using the position of the sun or stars to tell direction. [12]Many species seem to have genetically programmed information about the direction of the sun at various times of day, and also possess a biological clock that measures off a roughly twenty-four-hour day. [13]Other birds have the remarkable ability to "read" the night sky. [14]Indigo buntings, for example, seem to have a built-in star map that enables them to find north during spring migration by looking at the stars.

____ 1. In sentence 4, the word *cues* means
    A. visual clues.
    B. movements.
    C. suggestions.
    D. lines.

____ 2. The digger wasp used the pine cones as
    A. protection.
    B. food.
    C. a way to attract a mate.
    D. a marker by which to find her nest.

____ 3. To find their way, birds may use
    A. rivers and seashores.
    B. the position of the sun.
    C. the position of the stars.
    D. all of the above.

____ 4. The relationship of the second paragraph to the first is one of
    A. addition.
    B. time.
    C. contrast.
    D. cause and effect.

(Continues on next page)

_____ 5. The indigo bunting is a type of
   A. star.
   B. bird.
   C. insect.
   D. built-in star map.

_____ 6. We can conclude from the passage that the digger wasp gets its name from
   A. its shape.
   B. the person who first discovered it.
   C. the way it moves.
   D. the way it creates its nest.

_____ 7. The passage suggests that
   A. all animals have the same abilities.
   B. digger wasps can solve problems logically.
   C. birds have senses that humans do not have.
   D. all of the above.

_____ 8. Which is the most appropriate title for this passage?
   A. The Lives of Insects and Birds
   B. Telling Direction by the Sun and Stars
   C. Animal Parents
   D. How Animals Use Vision to Find Their Way

_____ 9. The main idea of the passage is stated in
   A. sentence 1.
   B. sentence 2.
   C. sentence 9.
   D. sentence 10.

_____10. The passage
   A. lists examples of the main idea.
   B. shows causes for the main idea.
   C. defines and illustrates a term.
   D. presents all of the major details in time order.

COMBINED SKILLS: Test C

After reading the textbook passage, write the letter of the best answer to each question.

¹On the eve of Halloween in 1938, a twenty-three-year-old radio producer and actor, Orson Welles, broadcast his rendition of H.G. Wells's novel *The War of the Worlds* on the *Mercury Theatre on the Air.*

²All week the cast had been struggling to adapt the story to radio and was finding it difficult to make the drama believable. ³So Welles decided to present the story as an interruption of a regular music broadcast, with news reporters breathlessly cutting in to describe the landing of creatures from Mars.

⁴Although the broadcast included four announcements that the attack was just a dramatization, many people were listening to the Edgar Bergen and Charlie McCarthy show on another network when *The War of the Worlds* began. ⁵During the first commercial on the McCarthy program, many people turned the dial to see what else was on. ⁶They tuned in to an announcer describing a strange creature climbing out of a vessel in Grovers Mill, New Jersey. ⁷Then they heard the announcer and a crowd of people being annihilated by the creature's ray gun. ⁸National panic set in as people telephoned friends and relatives to warn them of the impending disaster.

⁹By the end of the hour-long broadcast, people had attempted suicide, jammed long-distance telephone lines and caused national uproar. ¹⁰Military personnel were called back to their bases. ¹¹In Concrete, Washington, a power failure during the broadcast caused a traffic jam as most of the town's residents fled in their automobiles to escape the invading Martians.

____ 1. In sentence 1, the word *rendition* means
   A. memory.
   B. review.
   C. version.
   D. preview.

____ 2. In sentence 7, the word *annihilated* means
   A. eaten.
   B. destroyed.
   C. ignored.
   D. strengthened.

____ 3. Welles's radio show was based on a
   A. play.
   B. folktale.
   C. biography.
   D. novel.

(Continues on next page)

____ 4. According to the passage, the broadcast of *The War of the Worlds* included
  A. no commercials.
  B. four commercials.
  C. actual news reporters.
  D. four announcements that the story was fictional.

____ 5. The relationship between the two parts of sentence 5 is one of
  A. time.
  B. addition.
  C. contrast.
  D. comparison.

____ 6. The relationship of sentence 7 to the sentence before it is one of
  A. time.
  B. addition.
  C. contrast.
  D. illustration.

____ 7. The main pattern of organization of the passage is
  A. list of items.
  B. time order.
  C. definition and example.
  D. comparison and/or contrast.

____ 8. The passage clearly implies that the *Mercury Theater on the Air*
  A. was more popular than the Edgar Bergen and Charlie McCarthy show.
  B. wasn't very popular at all.
  C. specialized in science fiction.
  D. was broadcast nationally.

____ 9. We can conclude that many people felt Welles
  A. should never have tried to dramatize *The War of the Worlds*.
  B. should have appeared instead on the Edgar Bergen and Charlie McCarthy show.
  C. had no talent for radio.
  D. made the drama too believable.

____10. Which statement best expresses the main idea of this passage?
  A. A realistic radio drama about alien invaders caused national panic and uproar.
  B. Orson Welles presented a radio version of *The War of the Worlds*.
  C. Some people who tuned in to the *War of the Worlds* broadcast after it had already begun missed the announcement that it was just a dramatization.
  D. After a power failure in one Washington town, most residents fled to escape the Martians they thought were coming.

COMBINED SKILLS: Test D

After reading the textbook passage, write the letter of the best answer to each question.

¹College classrooms are often drab and dreary places. ²Walls are painted a variation of "institutional gray"; furniture is easy to clean, but uncomfortable and unattractive. ³Chairs are lined up in straight rows facing the teacher's desk or lectern. ⁴In one study, over 80 percent of university students rated their classrooms negatively, describing them as ugly, cramped, stuffy, and uncomfortable. ⁵Research by environmental psychologists is beginning to show that unattractive classrooms are not only unappealing; they may also adversely affect academic performance.

⁶A more carefully controlled study of classroom environments was conducted by Wolling and Montage (1981). ⁷They selected two identical classrooms located side by side in the psychology building. ⁸The control classroom, which they called the "sterile classroom," had white walls, a gray carpet, and rows of plastic desks. ⁹The experimental classroom, which they called the "friendly classroom," was redecorated with the help of a design consultant. ¹⁰Several walls were painted bright colors, art posters were hung on the walls, large plants were added to the room, and colorful Chinese kites were hung from the ceiling. ¹¹In addition to traditional desks, a part of the room was outfitted with area rugs, color-coordinated cushions, and wooden cubes to provide nontraditional seating.

¹²The researchers investigated how these two different environments affected performance in actual college classes. ¹³Two professors teaching introductory psychology agreed to participate in the study although they were not informed of the purpose of the research. ¹⁴When school began, each class was randomly assigned to one of the two rooms. ¹⁵Halfway through the term, the classes switched rooms. ¹⁶Thus students in both classes spent half the term in the control room and half in the "friendly" room. ¹⁷Students were not told they were being studied; the switch in rooms was explained as occurring because the original room was needed for videotaping.

¹⁸The most striking finding from this study was that students performed significantly better on regular course exams when they were in the friendly rather than the sterile classroom.

_____ 1. In sentence 5, the word *adversely* means
   A. never.
   B. helpfully.
   C. negatively.
   D. playfully.

_____ 2. In sentence 8, the word *sterile* means
   A. free of germs.
   B. empty.
   C. lifeless.
   D. safe.

(Continues on next page)

_____ 3. The "friendly classroom" had
    A. bright walls.
    B. calm, pale colors.
    C. white walls.
    D. wall-to-wall carpeting.

_____ 4. The students in the study
    A. helped design the "friendly classroom."
    B. took two different courses.
    C. stayed in one room throughout the course.
    D. were not told they were involved in a study.

_____ 5. The main pattern of organization of the second paragraph is
    A. time order.
    B. definition and example.
    C. cause and effect.
    D. comparison and/or contrast.

_____ 6. TRUE OR FALSE? Wolling and Montage's study was concerned with a cause-effect relationship.

_____ 7. The passage implies that the "friendly classroom" was designed to be
    A. cheerful.
    B. informal.
    C. comfortable.
    D. all of the above.

_____ 8. We can conclude from the passage that the two professors might have guessed the purpose of the study they were in because
    A. they had read about the interests of the two researchers.
    B. one of the two rooms they taught in was decorated unusually.
    C. someone gave them hints about the purpose.
    D. the study was done many times before.

_____ 9. Which would be the most appropriate title for this passage?
    A. Traditional Desks versus Cushions and Wooden Cubes
    B. Sterile and Friendly Classrooms
    C. An Unusual Psychology Course
    D. Color in the Classroom

_____ 10. The main idea of the passage is best expressed in
    A. sentence 4.
    B. sentence 5.
    C. sentence 7.
    D. sentence 17.

ANSWERS TO THE TESTS IN THE FIRST TEST BANK

VOCABULARY IN CONTEXT: Test A

1. Examples: *paying the telephone bill, picking up the groceries;* B
2. Examples: *eating with my hands, being late everywhere I go;* B
3. Examples: *his car broke down, he lost his wallet, his computer crashed and he lost a day's work;* D
4. basic
5. requirement
6. shortage
7. Antonym: *wild;* A
8. Antonym: *poor;* C
9. D
10. A

VOCABULARY IN CONTEXT: Test B

1. Examples: *travel TV shows, magazines;* C
2. Examples: *keeps them from exercising, encourages them to eat unhealthy foods, teaches them to be violent;* D
3. outdated
4. wiped out
5. threat
6. Antonym: *silent;* B
7. Antonym: *hidden;* A
8. Antonym: *grow;* C
9. D
10. B

VOCABULARY IN CONTEXT: Test C

1. B	6. A
2. C	7. B
3. B	8. C
4. C	9. A
5. D	10. D

VOCABULARY IN CONTEXT: Test D

1. C	6. A
2. B	7. B
3. D	8. A
4. D	9. A
5. C	10. D

MAIN IDEAS: Test A

1. 2	4. 1
2. 1	5. 3
3. 7	

MAIN IDEAS: Test B

1. 2	4. 1
2. 3	5. 2
3. 5	

MAIN IDEAS: Test C

1. 2	4. 2
2. 1	5. 1
3. 7	

MAIN IDEAS: Test D

1. 2	4. 1
2. 1	5. 3
3. 6	

SUPPORTING DETAILS: Test A

A.
1. D	4. C
2. C	5. D
3. A	6. Herbivorous (plants)

B. (7–10.) *Main idea:* . . . categories of burn injuries.
1. First-degree—leave a painful red mark but do not break the skin so do not often become infected
2. Second-degree
3. Third-degree—outer and inner layers of skin are burned, causing little pain but possibility of serious or even fatal infection

SUPPORTING DETAILS: Test B

A.
1. B	4. C
2. D	5. C
3. C	

B. (6–10.) *Main idea:* . . . genetic factors.
2. Intellectual traits
   Examples—scores on intelligence tests, memory
3. Personality factors
   Examples—shyness and special talents and interests

Note: Wording of main ideas and supporting details in Tests A–D may vary.

SUPPORTING DETAILS: Test C

A. (1–4.) *Main idea:* Psychologists use several theories to explain human behavior.
   • Psychoanalytic theory holds that people are driven by "subconscious" needs and desires.
   • Behaviorism suggests that people's actions are based on past experiences of reward and punishment.
   • . . . the role of overall patterns in our thinking.

B. 5. 2   8. constructive
   6. B   9–10. 1. Constructive forces, which lift up land masses
   7. C   2. a. Cutting action of running streams

SUPPORTING DETAILS: Test D

A. (1–6.) *Main idea:* Reasons poor people are less healthy than well-off people
   • Less nutritious diets
   • Lower standard of living
   • Less or lower-quality medical care
   • Physical stress
   • Psychological stress

B. 7. 1   9. B
   8. B   10. B

IMPLIED MAIN IDEAS/CENTRAL POINT: Test A

A. 1. A   B. 4. Sentence 1
   2. C
   3. B

IMPLIED MAIN IDEAS/CENTRAL POINT: Test B

A. 1. B   B. 4. Sentence 2
   2. C
   3. C

IMPLIED MAIN IDEAS/CENTRAL POINT: Test C

A. 1. B
   2. D
B. 3. Women use more flirting techniques than men do. *Note: Wording of answer may vary.)*
C. 4. Sentence 7

IMPLIED MAIN IDEAS/CENTRAL POINT: Test D

A. 1. A
   2. D
B. 3. Several facts about the monarch butterfly are a mystery to scientists. *(Wording may vary.)*
C. 4. Sentence 13

RELATIONSHIPS I: Test A

A. 1. after   B. 6. One
   2. until   7. Another
   3. next   8. during
   4. also   9. third
   5. Another   10. A

RELATIONSHIPS I: Test B

A. 1. B   B. 6. A
   2. A   7. then
   3. B   8. As
   4. A   9. Finally
   5. A   10. B

RELATIONSHIPS I: Test C

A. 1. B   C. • Notorious criminal cases that get heavy news coverage
   2. Soon *or* Eventually *or* thcn   • Other serious felonies that get less news coverage
B. 3. A   *Examples*—murders, rapes, robberies
   4. B   • Less serious felonies that may not get prison terms
   5–6. 1. They make and use tools.   • Misdemeanors *Example*—traffic violations
       2. They eat meat regularly.

RELATIONSHIPS I: Test D

A. 1. A   C. 7. B
   2. moreover   8–10. *Main idea:* . . . five stages
B. 3. A   • Stage 3: chronic exhaustion, physical illness, anger, depression
   4. 1
   5. furthermore   • Stage 5: "Professional burnout"—alcoholism, drug abuse, heart disease
   6. C

RELATIONSHIPS II: Test A

A.
1. for example
2. However
3. reason
4. Despite
5. similar

B.
6. A
7. C
8. B
9. A
10. C

RELATIONSHIPS II: Test B

A.
1. B
2. reason *or* causing

B.
3. C
4. same *or* despite *or* differences *or* similar

C.
5. A
6. for example

D.
7. B
8. result *or* effects *or* because

E.
9. C
10. opposite *or* different

RELATIONSHIPS II: Test C

A.
1. C
2. B

B.
3. A
4. A

B.
5. C

C.
6. B

7–10.
- Seek to escape conflict at home
- Overwhelmed by demands of adult life
- Want to commit to establishment of a better world

Main idea: . . . cults for several common reasons.

RELATIONSHIPS II: Test D

A.
1. B

2–4. *Main idea:* . . . common causes of a small business's failure.
- Neglect
- Weak control systems

B.
5. 1
6. C

7–10. *Heading:* Cities in Developing Countries
- Almost one half of population
- One quarter of work force unemployed

Homelessness

FACT AND OPINION: Test A

A.
1. F
2. F
3. O
4. F
5. O
6. O
7. F
8. O
9. O
10. F

B.
11. F
12. F+O
13. F+O
14. F+O
15. F

C.
16. F
17. F
18. O
19. F+O
20. O

FACT AND OPINION: Test B

A.
1. O
2. F
3. F
4. O
5. O
6. O
7. F
8. F+O
9. F
10. O

11. F
12. F+O

B.
13. O
14. F
15. F+O

C.
16. F
17. O
18. O
19. F
20. F

FACT AND OPINION: Test C

A.
1. F
2. F
3. O
4. O
5. F
6. F
7. O
8. F
9. F+O
10. F

11. O
12. F+O

B.
13. F
14. F
15. F
16. O

C.
17. F
18. F
19. O
20. F+O

FACT AND OPINION: Test D

A.
1. O
2. F
3. O
4. F
5. F
6. F+O
7. F
8. O
9. F
10. F+O

B.
11. F
12. F+O
13. F
14. F
15. O

C.
16. F
17. F
18. O
19. F
20. F+O

INFERENCES: Test A

A. 1. C   4. C
   2. B   5. B
   3. B
B. 2, 3, 4, 6, 8

INFERENCES: Test B

A. 1. A   B. 3. C
   2. C   4. B
C. 1, 2, 5, 6, 8, 10

INFERENCES: Test C

A. 1. C   3. B
   2. B   4. C
B. 1, 3, 5, 7, 8, 10

INFERENCES: Test D

A. 2, 3, 5, 7, 9, 10
B. 3, 7, 9, 10

PURPOSE AND TONE: Test A

A. 1. I   6. E
   2. P   7. P
   3. E   B. 8. C
   4. P   9. D
   5. I   10. A

PURPOSE AND TONE: Test B

A. 1. B   6. I
   2. C   7. J
   3. E   8. D
   4. F   B. 9. I
   5. H   10. P

PURPOSE AND TONE: Test C

A. 1. B   C. 5. B
   2. C   6. B
B. 3. A   D. 7. B
   4. D   8. A

PURPOSE AND TONE: Test D

A. 1. A   C. 5. C
   2. A   6. C
B. 3. B   D. 7. A
   4. C   8. C

ARGUMENT: Test A

A. 1. B   4. B
   2. B   B. 5–7. A, E, F
   3. C   8–10. A, B, E

ARGUMENT: Test B

A. 1. D   B. 4. D
   2. C   5. B
   3. B

ARGUMENT: Test C

A. 1–3. B, D, F   C. 8. B
   4–6. A, C, E   9. B
B. 7. C   10. C

ARGUMENT: Test D

A. 1–3. B, D, E   C. 8. C
   4–6. A, C, F   9. D
B. 7. A   10. C

COMBINED SKILLS: Test A

1. B   6. D
2. D   7. A
3. C   8. A
4. C   9. B
5. A   10. C

COMBINED SKILLS: Test B

1. A   6. D
2. D   7. C
3. D   8. D
4. A   9. A
5. B   10. A

COMBINED SKILLS: Test C

1. C   6. A
2. B   7. B
3. D   8. D
4. D   9. D
5. A   10. A

COMBINED SKILLS: Test D

1. C   6. T
2. C   7. D
3. A   8. B
4. D   9. B
5. D   10. B

Name _____

Section _____ Date _____

SCORE: (Number correct) × 10 = _____%

VOCABULARY IN CONTEXT: Test 1

Use context clues to choose the word closest in meaning to each capitalized word. Then write the letter of your choice.

____ 1. The teacher did not believe the student's IMPLAUSIBLE story that a burglar had stolen his research paper.
   A. unlikely   B. funny   C. impressive

____ 2. The baby DERIVES more pleasure from playing with the box that the toy came in than from the toy itself.
   A. causes   B. wishes for   C. gets

____ 3. Two great PERILS of working in coal mines are black lung disease and mine cave-ins.
   A. benefits   B. dangers   C. causes

____ 4. Aspirin usually ALLEVIATES my headaches, but sometimes only lying down and shutting my eyes relieves them.
   A. worsens   B. brings   C. eases

____ 5. You must work steadily with a dog to train it well. You won't succeed with only INTERMITTENT practice.
   A. constant   B. starting and stopping   C. very believable
                                       from time to time

____ 6. With the PROLIFERATION of new housing developments, our town suddenly needs more schools and wider roads.
   A. sudden decrease   B. rapid increase   C. standing still

____ 7. The path follows the river for a mile and then DIVERGES into two paths, one that stays with the river and one that goes north.
   A. reduces   B. remains   C. branches out

____ 8. My brother is such an AVID fan of Gloria Estefan that his bedroom walls are covered with posters of her, and he has bought all of her record albums.
   A. enthusiastic   B. temporary   C. threatening

____ 9. A computer FACILITATES writing a paper by greatly simplifying the process of revising.
   A. confuses   B. makes easier   C. slows down

____ 10. Although the law requires us to DISCLOSE everything we earn on our tax returns, many people hide a portion of their earnings from the Internal Revenue Service.
   A. conceal   B. make known   C. pay

TEN STEPS TO IMPROVING
COLLEGE READING SKILLS

Note: This test is identical to the Townsend Press Software Test 2 on Vocabulary in Context.

Name _____

Section _____ Date _____

SCORE: (Number correct) × 10 = _____%

VOCABULARY IN CONTEXT: Test 2

Use context clues to choose the word closest in meaning to each capitalized word. Then write the letter of your choice.

____ 1. Boaters should know the OMINOUS signs of an approaching storm, such as increasingly dark clouds and rapidly changing wind directions.
    A. threatening   B. doubtful   C. cheerful

____ 2. While many people believe that capital punishment is a DETERRENT to crime, murder rates have not gone down in states that have the death penalty.
    A. encouragement   B. foundation   C. discouragement

____ 3. One of the kidnappers ELUDED the FBI's roadblock, but two other suspects were caught.
    A. ran into   B. escaped   C. saw

____ 4. During America's Great Depression, unemployment was PREVALENT. Over twelve million people were out of work by 1932.
    A. unlikely   B. old-fashioned   C. widespread

____ 5. Learning that their son had cancer DEVASTATED the Millers.
    A. annoyed   B. greatly upset   C. endangered

____ 6. Jim wouldn't DIVULGE where he was taking Lisa on her birthday, saying only, "It's a surprise."
    A. avoid   B. accept   C. reveal

____ 7. After all the BLAND hospital food, a spicy taco seemed very appealing.
    A. mild   B. rich   C. sharp

____ 8. If your best friend won't give you a CANDID answer, then whom should you go to for an honest response?
    A. false   B. sincere   C. long

____ 9. Household injuries can occur even during the most MUNDANE activities, such as bathing, ironing and cooking.
    A. unusual   B. difficult   C. ordinary

____ 10. The band's early concert tours proved more popular than the SUBSEQUENT oncs.
    A. first   B. later   C. unexpected

TEN STEPS TO IMPROVING
COLLEGE READING SKILLS

Note: This test is identical to the Townsend Press Software Test 1 on Main Ideas.

Name _____

Section _____ Date _____

SCORE: (Number correct) × 10 = _____%

MAIN IDEAS: Test 1

Each of the following groups of statements includes one main idea and two supporting details. In the space provided, write the letter of each main idea.

____ *Group 1*

    A. Doris likes doing detail work.

    B. Doris should consider becoming a bookkeeper.

    C. Doris always did well in math.

____ *Group 2*

    A. Six hundred people died in the San Francisco earthquake in 1906.

    B. The earthquake left 300,000 homeless.

    C. The San Francisco earthquake of 1906 was terribly destructive.

____ *Group 3*

    A. A government survey of eating habits shows many people's diets are unbalanced.

    B. About two out of every five people ate no fruits.

    C. More than four out of every five had no high-fiber bread or cereal in their diet.

____ *Group 4*

    A. The Smithsonian contains an ancient Chinese scroll and Ray Bolger's *Wizard of Oz* scarecrow costume.

    B. Also stored there are a giant Pacific octopus and thousands of World's Fair souvenirs dating to 1850.

    C. The Smithsonian Institution, based in Washington, D.C., stores an odd assortment of interesting items.

____ *Group 5*

    A. The Romans believed that eating garlic gives strength and courage.

    B. Throughout the ages, people have believed that garlic has special powers.

    C. During the Middle Ages, wearing garlic was thought to protect people against werewolves and vampires.

____ *Group 6*

    A. Washoe, a female chimpanzee who was taught sign language, has created some words on her own.

    B. Washoe thought up the term "drink-fruit" for watermelon.

    C. Washoe, who has called an enemy "dirty Jack," calls the swan "water-bird."

(Continues on next page)

_____ *Group 7*

A. The sand-dune cat seems to get along without drinking by getting enough liquid from the bodies of the animals it eats.
B. The sand-dune cat is well suited for the deserts it lives in.
C. The sand-dune cat's feet are thickly padded, which helps it walk over sand.

_____ *Group 8*

A. Smoking is highly addictive, some say as addictive as heroin.
B. Smoking is a common social habit. Some smokers don't feel comfortable at a party without a cigarette.
C. There are several reasons why people still smoke.

_____ *Group 9*

A. Animal research in Japan suggests that ginger can suppress coughs and reduce fever and pain.
B. Some studies have shown that ginger has various health benefits.
C. One study found that powdered ginger was very effective in blocking motion sickness.

_____ *Group 10*

A. Rain-forest trees are cut down for their timber faster than new trees can grow to replace them.
B. The rain forests of the world, home to plants and animals still unknown to science, are being carelessly destroyed.
C. Even though the nutrients in rain-forest soil are quickly used up in farming, farmers burn down the forests to plant crops.

TEN STEPS TO IMPROVING
COLLEGE READING SKILLS

Name _____

Section _____ Date _____

SCORE: (Number correct) × 10 = _____%

Note: This test is identical to the Townsend Press Software Test 2 on Main Ideas.

MAIN IDEAS: Test 2

In the space provided, write the number of the sentence that expresses the main idea in each selection.

_____ 1. [1]When a female elephant gives birth, she is often helped by another female from the herd. [2]This "friend" may actually help deliver the baby with her trunk and often washes the newborn. [3]The females take turns "babysitting" the young of the herd while the other mothers eat. [4]Elephants care for one another when they are ill. [5]They have been known to take food and water to sick herdmates for many weeks. [6]Elephants also tend to the dying. [7]They will often surround a dying elephant, trying to lift it back on its feet; and if it dies, they will stay sadly with the body for some time and even attempt to bury it. [8]Because of these and other behaviors, the elephant has earned the reputation as one of the most intelligent animals.

_____ 2. [1]A car is stolen somewhere in this country every thirty-seven seconds. [2]Despite this fact, you can use a few simple precautions to prevent theft. [3]You can avoid tempting thieves by locking all valuables in the trunk or glove compartment. [4]Also, you can discourage thieves with tow trucks by parking in the middle of a block on a busy, well-lit street. [5]And last, don't forget the obvious precaution of locking the car and taking your keys—even if you're stopping just for a minute. [6]One out of every five stolen cars was left unlocked with the keys in the ignition.

_____ 3. [1]Have you ever read an entire page of something only to turn to the next page and realize you have no idea of what you just read? [2]Such absent-minded reading is something we all do at one time or another. [3]Luckily, there are ways to conquer this habit of reading on automatic pilot. [4]Highlighting passages—underlining or using a highlighter pen—is one way to involve yourself more in the reading process. [5]Another, more unusual way to focus your attention on what you're reading is to read while standing. [6]To improve his concentration, John F. Kennedy often read while standing at a lectern.

_____ 4. [1]Scientists have discovered that the sensory stimuli of our sleeping environment may intrude into our dreams. [2]A particular odor or the telephone's ringing may be instantly and creatively woven into the dream story. [3]In one experiment, some researchers lightly sprayed cold water on dreamers' faces. [4]Compared with sleepers who did not get the cold-water treatment, these subjects were more likely to dream about water—about waterfalls, about leaky roofs, or even about being sprayed by someone.

_____ 5. [1]Small animals eat more in relation to their own size than large animals do. [2]For instance, a field mouse eats as much as its own body weight every day. [3]That is, a one-ounce mouse will eat one ounce of food a day, or 100 percent of its body weight. [4]However, an elephant that may weigh twelve thousand pounds will eat about six hundred pounds of food a day. [5]As astounding an amount of food as that is to eat, it is still only 5 percent (or 1/20th) of the elephant's body weight.

(Continues on next page)

_____ 6. [1]Dog walking often involves taking solitary journeys, sometimes after dark. [2]As a result, it can leave you prey to muggers and other criminals. [3]But there are some simple ways to protect yourself from predators while walking your dog. [4]First, follow your instincts, not your animal's. [5]Dogs automatically head for bushes and parks—but so do potential attackers. [6]As much as possible, stick to busy, well-lit streets, which discourage criminal activity. [7]Also, consider buying a retractable leash, which rolls in and out like a measuring tape. [8]Keep your dog as close to you as possible—but if he insists on relieving himself in a dark or isolated spot, lengthen the leash, so you can stay under a street light.

_____ 7. [1]We often say that "you get what you pay for." [2]However, a higher price does not always mean better quality. [3]For example, the perfume sold in an expensive shop may be exactly the same as the brand sold in a dime store, except for a fancy box and label— and a much higher price. [4]Customers pay the high price because they assume they are getting something special. [5]Similarly, the more expensive models of many cars are only slightly different from the basic model. [6]A few "extras" can be responsible for adding thousands of dollars to the price of the car.

_____ 8. [1]Sociologists have several basic methods of doing research. [2]First is the experiment, which is useful for clearly defined questions in which varying factors can be controlled. [3]Sociologists also use the survey, which is useful for gaining facts about a particular group; in order to be sound, the survey must be random. [4]Direct observation is helpful for in-depth studies of social processes, but to be useful, such observation must be made by a skilled researcher. [5]Finally, existing information can be studied as the basis for new conclusions.

_____ 9. [1]Psychologists have observed that some babies cry much more than others, and some are much more active than others. [2]Some are cuddly, and some seem to dislike being picked up and held. [3]Psychologists have also found that newborns are capable of expressing several basic emotions; for example, their faces show different expressions for surprise, distress, and disgust. [4]And they have their likes and dislikes: In one experiment, babies only a few hours old showed pleasure at the taste of sweetened water and smell of vanilla, but made faces at the taste of lemon juice and the smell of rotten eggs. [5]Through these findings, psychologists have confirmed what parents have always claimed to be true—that their babies seem to have distinctive personalities almost from birth.

_____ 10. [1]Some people think that all pit bulls are vicious. [2]But those pit bulls that are savagely aggressive have been trained in various ways to be so. [3]Some owners, for example, try to make their dogs more aggressive by forcing them to run on treadmills until they are exhausted. [4]Other training methods include putting collars of barbed wire on the dogs, feeding them live kittens or small dogs, and feeding them gunpowder or hot sauce. [5]In addition, some owners strengthen their pit bulls' jaws, already strong, by swinging the dogs from ropes while their teeth are clutching a tire.

TEN STEPS TO IMPROVING
COLLEGE READING SKILLS

*Note: This test is identical to the Townsend Press Software Test 1
on Supporting Details.*

Name _____

Section _____ Date _____

SCORE: (Number correct) × 10 = _____%

SUPPORTING DETAILS: Test 1

Write the letter of the number of major details in each selection. Notice that the main idea is **boldfaced** in each case.

___ 1. **These days most Americans get less than seven hours of sleep a night for reasons that are related to busy lifestyles.** One reason is that stress itself limits people's ability to sleep longer. Also, because many of the people who get under seven hours sleep are achievers, they simply don't have the time to sleep more.
   A. two major supporting details
   B. three major supporting details
   C. four major supporting details

___ 2. **People who want to cut down on salt should follow several steps.** First of all, they should read labels carefully. Ingredients to avoid include "sodium" and "monosodium glutamate." In addition, they should avoid salt-coated snacks. These include potato chips and pretzels. Finally, they should cook with onion or garlic powder instead of salt.
   A. two major supporting details
   B. three major supporting details
   C. four major supporting details

___ 3. A car is stolen somewhere in this country every thirty-seven seconds. **Despite this fact, you can use a few simple precautions to prevent theft.** You can avoid tempting thieves by locking all valuables in the trunk or glove compartment. Also, you can discourage thieves with tow trucks by parking in the middle of a block on a busy, well-lit street. And don't forget the obvious precaution of locking the car and taking your keys—even if you're stopping just for a minute. One out of every five stolen cars was left unlocked with the keys in the ignition.
   A. two major supporting details
   B. three major supporting details
   C. four major supporting details

___ 4. **You can avoid being ripped off by phony telephone pitches by following these guidelines.** First, be wary of high-pressure sales talk. Being pressured to buy on the spot is a clue that something isn't quite right—a legitimate business will give you time to consider its offer. Second, ask for the company's permanent address and phone number. A reliable company with nothing to hide shouldn't hesitate to give this information. Also, don't be overly impressed if you're offered a list of people who will "testify" as to how good the company's service or product is. Some businesses hire people to say these things. Last, if you are offered something that sounds too good to be true—such as a trip to Hawaii for only $50—it probably is not true.
   A. two major supporting details
   B. three major supporting details
   C. four major supporting details

(Continues on next page)

___ 5. Making a good first impression can lead to successful relationships in both love and work. **Here are some tips to ensure that you do begin relationships on the right foot.** First, dress appropriately for the occasion. Wearing at-home attire for a job interview, for example, can make the interviewer question your judgment and be unsure about hiring you. Next, be a good listener. This means not interrupting or monopolizing conversations. And remember that a good listener makes frequent eye contact. This will show you're "tuned in" to the other person and are not bored or distracted. Last, don't forget to smile. This will show you're a warm, cheerful person. Few folks like having gloomy types around, either at work or at play.

    A. two major supporting details
    B. three major supporting details
    C. four major supporting details

___ 6. **Throughout history, more than a few famous people were vegetarians.** For example, Pythagoras, the famous Greek mathematician who lived in the fifth century B.C., kept to a simple diet of bread, honey, and vegetables. Plato and Aristotle were also vegetarians. The poet Percy Bysshe Shelley became a convert to vegetarianism at twenty-one and later wrote a pamphlet in its defense. And Count Tolstoi, the Russian author famous for *War and Peace*, not only ate no animals; he would eat no eggs.

    A. three major supporting details
    B. four major supporting details
    C. five major supporting details

___ 7. **The consumer's attitudes toward an advertised product can go through several stages.** The first is simply lack of awareness, a total ignorance of a manufacturer's brand. From the manufacturer's point of view, this, of course, is the least desirable attitude. The next step up the ladder of success for the advertiser, therefore, is awareness. Simple awareness is followed by knowledge, a state in which the consumer has learned some facts about the product's advantages. A step above knowledge is acceptance, for that is the stage in which a consumer is as willing to buy a particular product as any other. When a shopper actually desires a product over competitors, that consumer has reached the preference stage. The final stage is insistence, which means the consumer will settle for no other product.

    A. four major supporting details
    B. five major supporting details
    C. six major supporting details

___ 8. **There are some common methods which people use to relieve stress in their lives.** The most common is to prepare for stress mentally. This includes several strategies, such as strengthening the resolve not to be bothered by certain things, pursuing a hobby, and listening to music. Another approach is to use some physical activity to relieve stress. Physical activities used in this way include exercise and breathing techniques. Yet another method for relieving stress is to make changes in one's social behavior, such as avoiding stressful social situations or seeking counseling in order to learn to minimize stress in relationships.

    A. three major supporting details
    B. five major supporting details
    C. ten major supporting details

(Continues on next page)

___ 9. **Sociologists have several basic methods of doing research.** First is the experiment, which is useful for clearly defined questions in which varying factors can be controlled. Sociologists also use the survey, which is useful for gaining facts about a particular group. In order to be sound, the survey must be random. Another method is direct observation, which is helpful for in-depth studies of social processes. To be useful, such observation must be made by a skilled researcher. Finally, existing information can be studied as the basis for new conclusions.
   A. three major supporting details
   B. four major supporting details
   C. five major supporting details

___ 10. **Most people are likely to respond to criticism in one of several ways.** They may withdraw when judged negatively by others and just accept criticism silently, without protest. They may even try to withdraw physically, by leaving the room or otherwise getting away from the critic. Another possible response is for people to try to justify themselves. They may spend hours or even days trying to come up with reasons that explain and legitimize their behavior. A third typical response to criticism is the counterattack. Here people try to reduce the pressure on themselves by attacking some fault or faults of the speaker. A counterattacker can sometimes appear to win a battle but wind up losing a friendship. A healthier response is to accept it in a positive way. People who react like this regard the criticism as an opportunity for self-examination and personal growth.
   A. two major supporting details
   B. three major supporting details
   C. four major supporting details

TEN STEPS TO IMPROVING
COLLEGE READING SKILLS

*Note: This test is identical to the Townsend Press Software Test 2
on Supporting Details.*

Name _____

Section _____ Date _____

SCORE: (Number correct) × 10 = _____%

SUPPORTING DETAILS: Test 2

Read each passage. Then write the letter of the correct answer to each supporting detail question.

A. A Japanese person who is embarrassed will not usually frown and look away as a Westerner might. Instead he or she will probably laugh. A Navajo Indian who is angry will not be likely to speak in a raised voice. He or she is more likely to speak extra quietly. And when a native of the Andaman Islands wants to show happiness upon the visit of a relative, he or she will not smile and embrace the visitor. Instead, the Andaman native will sit in the visitor's lap and cry. These responses demonstrate the fact that displays of emotion and their meaning vary greatly from culture to culture.

___ 1. In general, the major supporting details of this paragraph are
   A. reasons.
   B. statistics.
   C. examples.

___ 2. A Navajo Indian who is angry is likely to
   A. laugh.
   B. sit in someone's lap and cry.
   C. speak quietly.

B. You can influence the resale value of a car when you purchase it and while you use it. The most important element in pricing a used auto is the depreciation rate. This figure is found in consumer manuals for cars of the same model and age. By learning depreciation rates, you can buy a car that depreciates less than others. Since mileage is the next important consideration, you should try to stick to the average twelve thousand miles per year in a car you hope to sell eventually. Used-car buyers naturally are also concerned about the mechanical condition of a car, so it pays to do regular maintenance. Finally, the appearance of the car's body and interior affect its value, so it's important to avoid rust and dents and to keep the inside clean.

___ 3. In general, the major supporting details of this paragraph are
   A. depreciation rates.
   B. ways to care for your car so as to maintain a high resale value.
   C. things to do when purchasing and using a car that lead to a high resale value.

___ 4. The second sentence of the passage provides
   A. the main idea.
   B. a major detail.
   C. a minor detail.

(Continues on next page)

C. The names of many people, real and fictional, have become permanent parts of the language. General Ambrose Everett Burnside, for one, is remembered because of his long side whiskers—the Civil War-era general lent his name, with its syllables reversed, to the word *sideburns*. Another "person" whose name has been adopted into the language is that of Atlas, a giant from Greek mythology who supported the heavens on his shoulders. An early collection of maps had a picture of Atlas holding up the world, and *atlas* has come to mean any book of maps. Still another name-turned-word is based on Sir Robert Peel, the founder of the London (England) Metropolitan Police. London policemen are still called *bobbies* in honor of Sir Robert.

_____ 5. In general, the major details of this paragraph are
    A. examples of famous people.
    B. examples of English words based on fictional names.
    C. examples of names that have turned into English words.

_____ 6. Specifically, the major details of this paragraph are
    A. long side whiskers; Atlas holding up the world; Sir Robert Peel.
    B. General Burnside; Atlas; Sir Robert Peel.
    C. reversed syllables; a giant from Greek mythology; the London (England) Metropolitan Police.

D. How do we respond when painful or unpleasant things happen to us—if, for example, we are "dumped" by a girlfriend or boyfriend? We may react in either of two basic ways, which psychologists call suppression and repression. By suppression, psychologists mean a deliberate attempt to take our minds off the painful experience. We may start working twelve hours a day, for instance, hoping to keep too busy to feel the hurt. This technique seldom works for very long, though. The other mental defense, repression, is an unconscious effort to escape painful thoughts. We may start going to singles bars every night, go on a diet, or change the way we dress. Or we may start saying that the whole dating "scene" is stupid or immoral. These can all be ways that our unconscious tries to hide the pain of rejection.

_____ 7. In general, the major details are
    A. unpleasant things that happen to us.
    B. ways of working.
    C. basic ways we respond to unpleasant things that happen to us.

_____ 8. Specifically, the major details are
    A. working long hours; changes in dating behavior.
    B. suppression; repression.
    C. being "dumped" by a girlfriend; being "dumped" by a boyfriend.

(Continues on next page)

E. The number of trumpeter swans declined greatly between 1700 and the early 1900s. The main problem was hunters who sold the swans' feathers for hats, pens, pillows, and powder puffs. The Hudson Bay Company's records show that between 1823 and 1880 alone, 108,000 swan skins—mostly trumpeter—were sold in London. Beginning in the late 1800s, the trumpeter swan's population was also reduced by habitat destruction. This was mainly the result of farmers draining wetlands. By 1932, only 69 trumpeters were found in the lower 48 states.

___ 9. In general, the major supporting details of the passage are
    A. causes for the decline in the number of trumpeter swans.
    B. reasons why the trumpeter swans feathers were so popular.
    C. types of trumpeter swans.

___ 10. Specifically, the major details of the passage are
    A. people wanted the swans' feathers; people wanted their skins.
    B. the Hudson Bay company; the London market.
    C. people killed the swans for their feathers; people damaged the swans' environment.

TEN STEPS TO IMPROVING
COLLEGE READING SKILLS

*Note: This test is identical to the Townsend Press Software Test 1
on Implied Ideas/Central Point.*

Name _____

Section _____ Date _____

SCORE: (Number correct) × 10 = _____%

IMPLIED MAIN IDEA/CENTRAL POINT: Test 1

In the space provided, write the letter of the implied main idea of each selection.

_____ 1. Malcolm Muggeridge visited Mother Teresa in Calcutta after interviewing her for the BBC. "The thing I noticed about you and the hundreds of sisters who now form your team is that you all look so happy. Is it a put-on?" he asked. "Oh no," she replied, "not at all. Nothing makes you happier than when you really reach out in mercy to someone who is badly hurt."

As if to test Mother Teresa's idea, psychologist Bernard Rimland did an experiment. He asked 216 students to list the initials of ten people they knew best, yielding a grand list of some 2,000 people. He then asked them to indicate whether each person seemed happy or not. Finally, he asked them to go over each name again, indicating if the person seemed selfish (devoted mostly to his or her own welfare) or unselfish (willing to be inconvenienced for others). The striking result: 70 percent of those judged unselfish seemed happy; 95 percent of those judged selfish seemed unhappy.

A. Through studies, psychologists can learn a great deal about human nature.
B. It seems that unselfish people tend to be happier than selfish people.
C. Through her good works, Mother Teresa not only makes others happier; she makes herself happy.

_____ 2. High-school history teacher Bruce Janu makes smart alecks and troublemakers listen to Frank Sinatra. After that, the students usually don't mess with Janu again. "Some of the kids sit there and make faces when I'm playing Frank," said Janu, of Riverside High near Chicago. Janu said that his misbehaving students, who grew up on the wailing guitars of Megadeth and Pearl Jam, sometimes beg for mercy when they hear Old Blue eyes crooning "My Way" or "New York, New York."

In the old days, Joseph Cifelli, the principal of Cedarbrook Middle School in Cheltenham Township, Pennsylvania, said students caught fistfighting would automatically get a three-day suspension. But in this new era, where teachers see no point to sending students home to watch MTV, offenders have to report to the "Nature Center." There, they are charged with caring for a greenhouse of plants and animals ranging from an alligator to a finch. "The kids who are fighting have to talk it out there," said Cifelli, "and the plants and animals have a calming effect on them."

A. Music and greenhouses are becoming increasingly important in public education.
B. Frank Sinatra doesn't appeal to young students.
C. Educators are trying new ways of disciplining students.

_____ 3. What do you think about Harvey? He's handsome, hardworking, intelligent, and honest. He's also very conceited.

Did the last quality make a difference in your evaluation? If it did, you're not alone. Research shows that when people are aware of both the positive and negative characteristics of another person, they tend to be more influenced by the undesirable traits. In one study, for example, researchers found that job interviewers were likely to reject candidates who revealed negative information even when the total amount of information was highly positive.

Sometimes this attitude makes sense. If the negative quality clearly outweighs any positive ones, you'd be foolish to ignore it. A surgeon with shaky hands and a teacher who hates children, for example, would be unsuitable for their jobs whatever their other virtues.

(Continues on next page)

But much of the time it's a bad idea to pay excessive attention to negative qualities and overlook good ones. This is the mistake some people make when screening potential friends or dates: They find some who are too outgoing or too reserved, others who aren't intelligent enough, and still others who have the wrong sense of humor. Of course, it's important to find people you truly enjoy, but expecting perfection can lead to much unnecessary loneliness.

   A. Job interviewers tend to reject candidates who reveal negative information even if most of the information about the candidate was very positive.

   B. It can be difficult to find friends who have an intelligence and sense of humor like our own.

   C. We tend to be influenced more by people's negative traits than positive ones, an attitude that sometimes makes sense but often does not.

_____ 4. Merely sitting on the eggs does not insure the growth and hatching of the young birds. Feathers are insulation; to transmit heat to the eggs, birds develop "brood spots," bare patches on the underbody. The down falls out, the fat disappears and a concentration of blood vessels raises the temperature of the skin. Settling on the eggs, the bird parts its abdominal feathers and shimmies its body so that these spots come into comfortable contact with the eggs. In general these patches, numbering from one to three in different species, are present only in the sex that broods, or sits, on eggs; if both sexes share the labor, both have them. But not all birds have this thermostatic incubation aid. Ducks do not, but they compensate by pulling out the down themselves and adding it to the nest. Gannets do not have the patches either; they place a big webbed foot on the single egg, like a warming pad.

   A. There are various ways that birds keep their eggs warm enough.

   B. Brood spots are bare patches of the underbody which birds develop in order to keep their eggs at the proper temperature.

   C. Different members of the animal kingdom have differing ways of achieving the same goals.

_____ 5. When people in organizations are asked, "Which skills most need to be strengthened?" they often voice strong opinions. Several years ago, *Fortune* magazine surveyed many successful corporate executives to determine what subjects business schools should teach. The answer hits home: "Teach them to write better," said executive after executive. Another report indicates that "according to surveys of top officials in major American corporations, the greatest need among managers at all levels is to become more effective speakers and writers. . . . The time and money wasted—not to mention the clients lost—by poor writing are staggering in scope." Coopers & Lybrand, a prestigious accounting firm, is in such desperate need of good proposal writers that it has considered hiring English majors and providing them with on-the-job training in accounting.

   A. It appears that the country's schools are doing a poor job of educating students in all fields.

   B. *Fortune* magazine's survey of many business executives drew out strong opinions about business schools.

   C. The experience of business executives suggests that American business schools should do a better job of teaching communication skills.

_____ 6. The first stories were told before the first antelope were painted on cave walls. The first written literature grew from oral stories, as did great epic poems. Radio served as one of our principal storytellers until the arrival of television. Once TV arrived, however, words weren't good enough anymore. We needed lights, camera, action. TV told plenty of stories, all right, but it left little to the imagination. Eager for stories that can be seen on a mental screen, people are returning to the word. The revival began in the hills of Appalachia, where storytelling never really died out. "We're all storytellers," said Jimmy Neil Smith, executive director of the

(Continues on next page)

National Storytelling Association, which will hold its twenty-fifth-anniversary festival in Jonesborough this year. "We all live in a network of stories. There isn't a stronger connection between people than storytelling."

A. Radio and television serve the important need of providing society with storytellers.

B. There has been a revival of storytelling, a natural and important part of human life.

C. There are numerous helpful organizations in the country, including the National Storytelling Association.

_____ 7. James Laird and his colleagues indirectly got students to make a frowning expression—by asking them to "contract these muscles" and "pull your brows together" (supposedly to help the researchers attach facial electrodes). The results? The students reported feeling a little angry. Students similarly persuaded to smile felt happier, found cartoons more humorous, and recalled happier memories than did the frowners. People instructed to express other basic emotions also experienced them. For example, they reported feeling more fear than anger, disgust, or sadness when made to construct an expression of fear: "Raise your eyebrows. And open your eyes wide. Move your whole head back, so that your chin is tucked in a little bit, and let your mouth relax and hang open a little."

A. Researchers got students to frown by asking them to make the appropriate facial moves.

B. Laird's study shows that making a facial expression that corresponds with an emotion causes one to actually feel the emotion.

C. For a study, James Laird found ways to get people to make facial expressions that correspond to certain emotions.

_____ 8. In the middle of the nineteenth century, few buildings were higher than five stories. Church spires still dominated the urban skyline. Buildings, like cities themselves, were personal; they didn't dwarf the individual. That, however, soon changed. As a real estate columnist wrote in the *Chicago Tribune* in 1888: "In real estate calculations, Chicago has thus far had but three directions, north, south, and west, but there are indications now that a fourth is to be added and that it is to cut a larger figure in the coming decade than all the others. The new direction is zenithward. Since water hems in the business center on three sides and a nexus of railroads on the south, Chicago must grow upward."

Using traditional brick and masonry construction, architects could not design buildings much higher than ten stories. In 1885 New York architect William LeBaron Jenney solved the problem by using cast iron and steel. Using light masonry over an iron and steel skeleton, Jenney built the Home Insurance Building in Chicago, which although only ten stories was the first true skyscraper in history. Others soon followed. Steel, light masonry, and eventually glass revolutionized building construction.

A. The first skyscraper in history was designed by William LeBaron Jenney and built in Chicago in 1885 with light masonry and steel.

B. In the late 1800s, the personal size of the city was changed by skyscrapers, which became possible with new building materials and techniques.

C. Since few buildings were higher than five stories in the mid-1800s, the urban skyline was dominated then by church spires.

(Continues on next page)

_____ 9. Observational studies show that children imitate what they see and hear. The bad news from such studies is that antisocial models—in one's family or neighborhood, or on TV—may have antisocial effects. This helps us understand how abusive parents might have aggressive children and why men who batter their wives often had wife-battering fathers. The lessons we learn as children are not easily unlearned as adults, and they are sometimes visited on future generations.

The good news is that prosocial (positive, helpful) models can have prosocial effects. People who exemplify nonviolent, helpful behavior can prompt similar behavior in others. Mahatma Gandhi and Martin Luther King, Jr., both drew on the power of modeling, making nonviolent action a powerful force for social change. Parents are powerful models. European Christians who risked their lives to rescue Jews from the Nazis and American civil rights activists of a generation ago usually had a close relationship with at least one parent who modeled a strong moral or humanitarian concern.

A. The child's tendency to imitate explains why abusive parents have aggressive children and wife-batterers had wife-beating fathers.

B. Psychologists can learn a great deal about how people behave by observing them.

C. The behavior that children observe, whether antisocial or prosocial, influences their own behavior throughout their lives.

_____ 10. Individual businesspeople shaped the modern American city. They laid the horsecar and trolley lines, constructed the skyscrapers, apartments, and tenements, and provided water for the growing urban populations. Like their industrial counterparts, they worked, planned, and invested, fully expecting to earn huge profits. Their pocketbooks came before their civic responsibilities. The result was that they provided good housing and services for only those city dwellers who could pay. Allowing the profit motive to determine urban growth led to such waste and inefficiency as too many trolley lines (where businesses could make great profits) and such inconveniences as poorly cleaned streets (where businesses could make little profit). But most important, it stood contrary to planned urban growth. Urban businesspeople were generally unconcerned about the city as a whole. They regarded parks as uneconomic use of real estate and battled against the idea of zoning. In the end, they contributed to the ugliness and problems of Pittsburgh, New York, Chicago, and other American cities.

A. Many of the problems of America's cities stem from the fact that they were developed by businesspeople interested in profits.

B. The world's cities have not always been developed in the wisest ways.

C. Urban businesspeople provided high quality housing and services for those city residents who were able to pay for them.

TEN STEPS TO IMPROVING
COLLEGE READING SKILLS

Name _____

Section _____ Date _____

Note: This test is identical to the Townsend Press Software Test 2 on Implied Ideas/Central Point.

SCORE: (Number correct) × 10 = _____%

IMPLIED MAIN IDEA/CENTRAL POINT: Test 2

In the space provided, write the number of the sentence that expresses the central point in each selection.

_____ 1. [1]Prosocial behavior includes any act that helps or is designed to help others, regardless of the helper's motives. [2]Scientists have long observed prosocial behavior among animal species. [3]Charles Darwin (1871) noted that rabbits will make noise with their hind feet to warn other rabbits of predators. [4]In termite hives, the soldier termites will defend a nest against an intruder by putting themselves in front of the other termites and exposing themselves to great danger. [5]Many soldier termites die so that others may live and the nest survive. [6]Some varieties of baboons have a characteristic pattern of responding to threats. [7]The dominant males take the most exposed positions to protect the group and may even rush at an intruder. [8]As the tribe moves away from the threat, the males risk their own safety to remain behind to protect the rest of the group.

[9]Similarly, dolphins show a fascinating pattern of rescuing injured peers. [10]Since dolphins are mammals, they must breathe air to survive. [11]If an injured dolphin sinks below the surface, it will die. [12]Several observers have reported that dolphins will aid an injured companion. [13]In one case, a dolphin was stunned by an explosion in the water. [14]Two other adults came to its aid by holding the animals afloat until it recovered and was able to care for itself.

[15]Among many animals, parents will sacrifice themselves when their young are threatened. [16]An impressive example is the female nighthawk, which responds to a potential attack on her young by flying from the nest as if she had a broken wing, fluttering around at a low level, and finally landing on the ground right in front of the intruder but away from the nest.

_____ 2. [1]The notion that we should make a lifelong commitment to a single career is going out of style. [2]Not too long ago, students would choose a career and expect to stick with it. [3]Even today, professionals—physicians, lawyers, accountants, engineers, and college professors—start out assuming that they will spend their lives in one line of work. [4]In late adolescence and early adulthood, these people dedicate themselves to acquiring special skills and credentials. [5]Family, friends and associates also assume that they will spend their remaining years successfully pursuing a particular career. [6]That career is expected to provide a sense of achievement and fulfillment.

[7]Yet many people find these goals unattainable. [8]Seymour B. Sarason (1977) tracked the careers of some 2,300 individuals listed in *Who's Who*. [9]Roughly 40 percent of them had experienced a career shift. [10]And nearly 10 percent of the shifts represented a substantial movement from one area to another, such as from medicine to business or vice versa.

[11]Men and women may switch fields because they find that their career has not provided the fulfillment they had expected. [12]Or perhaps it has lost its challenge. [13]Others leave one career for another because they became bored, because they would like to give a new direction to their lives, or because they are having difficulty with their employer.

(Continues on next page)

_____ 3. [1]Stanford psychologist Philip Zimbardo recruited a group of middle-class, well-educated young men, all white except for one Asian. [2]He randomly chose eleven to serve as "guards" in a mock prison set up in the basement of Stanford's psychology building. [3]He issued the guards uniforms, handcuffs, whistles, and billy clubs. [4]The remaining ten subjects became "prisoners" and were placed in rooms with metal bars, bucket toilets, and cots.

[5]Zimbardo let the guards establish their own rules for the experiment. [6]The rules were tough: No talking during meals, rest periods, and after lights out. [7]Head counts at 2:30 a.m. [8]Troublemakers received short rations.

[9]Faced with these conditions, the prisoners began to resist. [10]Some barricaded their doors with beds. [11]Others went on hunger strikes. [12]Several ripped off their identifying number tags. [13]The guards reacted to the rebellion by clamping down hard on protesters. [14]Some turned sadistic, physically and verbally abusing the prisoners. [15]They threw prisoners into solitary confinement. [16]Others forced prisoners to call each other names and clean out toilets with their bare hands.

[17]Within a short time the experiment had become reality for both prisoners and guards. [18]Several inmates had stomach cramps and lapsed into uncontrollable weeping. [19]Others suffered from headaches, and one broke out in a head-to-toe rash after his request for early "parole" was denied by the guards.

[20]The experiment was scheduled to go on for two weeks, but after six days Zimbardo realized that what had started as a simulation had become too intense. [21]"I knew by then that they were thinking like prisoners and not like people," he said.

[22]This dramatic exercise in which twenty-one well-educated, middle-class citizens turned almost overnight into cruel bullies and discouraged victims tells us that how we think is a function of our roles in society.

_____ 4. [1]For a couple of reasons, we tend to like attractive people more than those considered unattractive. [2]One reason is the stereotype that a person who is physically attractive has other good qualities as well. [3]There is much evidence that attractive people are thought to be more socially skilled and friendly (but also more vain) than less attractive people.

[4]More surprising, attractive people are also seen to possess qualities that seem irrelevant to physical beauty, such as intelligence and mental health. [5]Here are just a few of the research findings: [6]Teachers evaluate cute children as being smarter and more popular than unattractive kids with identical academic records. [7]Students rate a lecture by a female teacher as being more interesting and judge the woman to be a better teacher if she is made up to look attractive rather than plain. [8]Even in the courtroom, attractive defendants sometimes receive more lenient sentences.

[9]A second reason for liking attractive people is the so-called radiating effect of beauty. [10]People may find it rewarding to be seen with a particularly attractive person because they think it will enhance their own public image.

_____ 5. [1]In A.D. 77, Pliny the Elder published the first encyclopedia, _Natural History_. [2]There are many factual explanations in the thirty-seven books of Pliny's encyclopedia. [3]However, there are also a good number of false ideas in Pliny's encyclopedia, some of which still linger in our legends, superstitions, folklore and mythologies. [4]Do porcupines shoot their quills? [5]No, but Pliny wrote that a porcupine "pierces the mouths of hounds when they close with it, and shoots out at them when further off," and the idea is still one of the most widespread zoological myths. [6]Do our ears ring when we're the subject of gossip? [7]There's no reason they should, but Pliny seemed to support that

(Continues on next page)

idea when he said it was an "accepted belief" that "absent people can divine by the ringing in their ears that they are the object of talk." ⁸Do hair and fingernails grow on a corpse? ⁹Pliny mentioned in passing that they do, and a hundred generations of boys and girls have repeated the story with delicious shudders of horror.

¹⁰In his calm authoritative voice, Pliny assures readers that various parts of the world are home to dog-headed people who communicate by barking; fast-running people whose feet are turned backward and have sixteen toes; people with feet so large that on hot days they lie on their backs with their feet in the air, shading them like umbrellas; people who are seven feet tall, never spit, and are exempt from toothaches and headaches; one-legged people who get around by hopping at great speed; headless, neckless people with eyes in their shoulders; and mouthless people who draw all of their nourishment from the scent of roots, flowers and apples and can be killed by offensive odors.

_____ 6. ¹Limestone and dolomite are carbonate rocks and are readily dissolved by water. ²In carbonate rock, channels or caves develop in places where water seeps along joints and faults. ³After a while, enough material is removed so that the overlying ground surface is no longer supported and the surface collapses or sinks, forming a sinkhole. ⁴Sinkholes present a real threat to health and property.

⁵Whereas topsoil filters bacteria out of water as it seeps through, water flowing directly into a sinkhole receives no filtering. ⁶As in a sewer, the underground flow in a sinkhole channel can carry pollution many miles. ⁷Untreated water from springs and wells in carbonate areas has been responsible for several outbreaks of typhoid fever. ⁸For example, in the 1940s in Tazewell, Tennessee, a typhoid fever outbreak due to contaminated water from a spring resulted in more than one hundred cases of illness, resulting in ten deaths.

⁹The collapse of sinkholes can swallow houses, highways, and cars and ruin cropland. ¹⁰Rubble and concrete are frequently dumped into sinkholes to try to stabilize them, sometimes to no avail. ¹¹When the ground is saturated with water, it gives some support; but the lowering of the groundwater table can bring on the collapse of the surface in an area prone to sinkholes. ¹²In 1981, an extended drought in Florida led to a rash of sinkholes—engulfing buildings, streets, and cars on automobile sales lots.

_____ 7. ¹The development of agriculture changed the world. ²No longer did humans wander the earth eking out a hand-to-mouth existence. ³They were able to settle in permanent locations and therefore could construct better shelters and accumulate possessions. ⁴More importantly, life ceased to be a constant struggle to find food.

⁵As time passed, the technology of agriculture improved. ⁶With each improvement, human society became more complex. ⁷The basis for this growing complexity was surplus food production. ⁸When a family could produce enough food to feed others as well as themselves, two new social phenomena became possible: specialization and urbanization.

⁹So long as everyone had to take part in the quest for food, no one could devote full time to other pursuits. ¹⁰Thus, during most of human existence, there were no full-time priests, political leaders, or other specialists. ¹¹But when farmers could produce some surplus, others could be supported who made their shoes, forged their tools, conducted their religious ceremonies, and guided their political affairs. ¹²Furthermore, people not needed for food production could congregate in a central place and thus create cities.

(Continues on next page)

_____ 8. [1]South central Nebraska, around the Prairie Bend region of the Platte River, provides a temporary home for some half a million sandhill cranes each spring. [2]Cranes arrive from the southern United States in early March and depart for northern nesting areas by mid-March. [3]During their stay in Nebraska, the cranes roost nightly on shallow sandbars in the Platte River to protect themselves from predators. [4]At dawn large flocks fly to the surrounding fields to feed on grain stubble left from the previous fall's harvest. [5]The flocks return to the roosting sites at dusk.

[6]The whole area has transmission lines of all sizes and heights, going in many directions. [7]Numerous crane collisions occur at some of the transmission lines.

[8]In the late 1980s, a study was conducted by the University of Wyoming to locate areas where there was high crane mortality from collisions with lines. [9]At nine such locations, yellow fiberglass aviation marking balls 30 centimeters in diameter (1 foot) with black stripes were installed at approximately 100-meter (109-yard) intervals on alternate spans. [10]A span is the section of wire between two support structures.

[11]After the installation, observers made daily observations of cranes found dead under the spans. [12]A significantly larger number of crane carcasses were found under unmarked spans. [13]Observation of flocks of cranes flying indicated that nearly half of the flocks reacted to the presence of the balls by increasing their altitude when approaching the marker. [14]Factors such as visibility and wind contributed to the reaction of cranes. [15]The study showed that in areas of numerous bird deaths from collisions with power lines, markers can be effective.

_____ 9. [1]People on a college campus were more likely to give money to the March of Dimes if they were asked for a donation by a paraplegic woman in a wheelchair than if asked by a nondisabled woman. [2]In another study, subway riders in New York saw a man carrying a cane stumble and fall to the floor. [3]Sometimes the victim had a large red birthmark on his face; sometimes he did not. [4]In this situation, the victim was more likely to receive aid if his face was unblemished (86 percent) than if he had an unattractive birthmark (61 percent). [5]In understanding these and other research findings, two themes are important: we are more willing to help people we like for some reason and people we think deserve assistance.

[6]In at least some situations, those who are physically attractive are more likely to receive aid. [7]For example, in a field study researchers placed a completed application to graduate school in a telephone booth at the airport. [8]The application was ready to be mailed, but had apparently been "lost." [9]The photo attached to the application was sometimes that of a very good-looking person and sometimes that of a less attractive person. [10]The measure of helping was whether the individual who found the envelope actually mailed it or not. [11]Results showed that people were more likely to send in the application if the person in the photo, whether male or female, was physically attractive.

[12]The degree of similarity between the potential helper and the person in need is also important. [13]For example, people are more likely to help a stranger who is from the same country rather than a foreigner. [14]In one study, shoppers on a busy street in Scotland were more likely to help a person wearing a plain T-shirt than a person wearing a T-shirt emblazoned with the prohomosexual slogan "GAY still means HAPPY."

[15]Whether a person receives help depends in part on the "merits" of the case. [16]For example, people in a supermarket were more likely to give someone money to buy milk rather than to buy cookie dough, presumably because milk is more essential for health than cookies. [17]Passengers on a New York subway were more likely to help a man who fell to the ground if he appeared to be sick rather than drunk.

(Continues on next page)

_____ 10. ¹Puritan sermons could last as long as two hours. ²Roman speakers of the second century took courses to improve their memory so that they could remember all that they had to say. ³Early American patriots spent the entire summer of 1787 debating the U.S. Constitution and then produced in its defense, for the newspapers of the day, eighty-five articles totaling nearly six hundred pages.

⁴Persuasion in modern times is quite different from that of earlier times in both length and timeliness. ⁵Today, a televised political advertisement typically runs for thirty seconds or less. ⁶Magazine ads often consist of little more than a picture and a phrase. ⁷As the columnist George Will once put it, if Lincoln were to give his Emancipation Proclamation today, he would probably say, "Read my lips. No more slavery." ⁸Our age of persuasion is populated with short, catchy, and often visually oriented messages.

⁹Persuasion in modern times is also much more immediate. ¹⁰The Puritan would wait all week for a sermon and months for news from England. ¹¹CNN coverage of the Tiananmen Square massacre stands in stark contrast. ¹²Despite efforts by the Chinese government to the contrary, journalists phoned in detailed reports of the violence, play-by-play descriptions of government action and student reaction, which were then quickly broadcast to an eagerly waiting but stunned world. ¹³In a similar vein, a week before the Allied bombing of Iraq in 1991, Tariq Aziz, foreign minister of Iraq, claimed to understand American politics because he got his news from CNN. ¹⁴The result is timely information—but, often perhaps, too timely. ¹⁵Whereas the Puritan could spend all week mulling over the implications of last Sunday's sermon, today's TV viewer and magazine reader has little time to think about one persuasive image before another one quickly takes its place.

TEN STEPS TO IMPROVING
COLLEGE READING SKILLS

*Note: This test is identical to the Townsend Press Software Test 1
on Relationships I.*

Name _____

Section _____ Date _____

SCORE: (Number correct) × 10 = _____%

RELATIONSHIPS I: Test 1

Read each item, and then answer the question about relationships in the space provided. Write in either the transition or the pattern of organization.

1. The garbage disposal has stopped working. Furthermore, the food trapped there is beginning to smell.

   The addition transition used is _____ *(write one word).*

2. After final exams are over, I plan to go home and sleep for a week.

   The time transition used is _____ *(write one word).*

3. Our landscaping is a mess. All of our old evergreen bushes are overgrown. Also, our front yard looks like a dandelion garden.

   The addition transition used is _____ *(write one word).*

4. When there's a huge sale going on at the mall, it's almost impossible to find a parking space there.

   The time transition used is _____ *(write one word).*

5. Thanksgiving is my favorite holiday because my whole family gets together then. In addition, we have all my favorite foods for dinner, including Aunt Lena's sweet-potato bread.

   The addition transition used is _____ *(write two words).*

6. First, dig a hole at least twice the width of the plant. Then mix some peat moss with soil at the bottom of the hole.

   The selection's main pattern of organization is _____
   *(write **list** or **time**).*

7. *The Book of Lists II* names "25 Things That Fell From The Sky." One was hay, which fell over the English town of Devizes at teatime on July 3, 1977. Another was black eggs, which were reportedly dropped by a heavy wind on Port-au-Prince, Haiti, on May 5, 1796.

   The selection's main pattern of organization is _____
   *(write **list** or **time**).*

8. One method of increasing your vocabulary is to list and look up all the unfamiliar words you find in a reading assignment. A second method is to buy a self-help vocabulary book and assign yourself one lesson a week.

   The selection's main pattern of organization is _____
   *(write **list** or **time**).*

   (Continues on next page)

9. Start building a fire by crumpling up wads of newspaper and placing them between the andirons. Then pile kindling wood on top of the newspaper. Next place several large logs on the andirons, leaving spaces between them so the fire can "breathe."

The selection's main pattern of organization is _____ (write **list** or **time**).

10. On the afternoon of July 20, l968, the lunar module, the *Eagle*, landed on the moon with astronauts Neil Armstrong and Edwin Aldrin. Six and a half hours after landing, the hatch of the *Eagle* was opened, and Armstrong began to descend a ladder to the surface of the moon.

The selection's main pattern of organization is _____ (write **list** or **time**).

TEN STEPS TO IMPROVING
COLLEGE READING SKILLS

Name _____

Section _____ Date _____

SCORE: (Number correct) × 10 = _____%

*Note: This test is identical to the Townsend Press Software Test 2
on Relationships I.*

RELATIONSHIPS I: Test 2

Read each item, and then answer the question about relationships in the space provided. Write in either the transition or the pattern of organization.

1. Make a paste of water and flour. Next, tear newspaper into many strips and dip the strips into the flour.

   The time transition used is _____ *(write one word).*

2. You need discipline to work well. You may also need discipline to play well.

   The addition transition used is _____ *(write one word).*

3. To start the washer, select the water temperature and push in the cycle-control knob toward the desired cycles and wash time. Finally, pull that knob out.

   The time transition used is _____ *(write one word).*

4. According to one expert, it's a sign that a marriage is headed for trouble if a couple is having difficulty finding time to be together. A second sign is if the couple no longer has fun together.

   The addition transition used is _____ *(write one word).*

5. When we were children, we could make a candy bar last for an entire movie.

   The time transition used is _____ *(write one word).*

6. Alaska's road to statehood involved a series of "owners." The original people to live in the huge state of Alaska were Eskimos, Aleuts (natives of the Aleutian Islands, which lie off of Alaska), and Indians. In 1731, a Russian explorer landed on the Alaskan coast. Russia claimed the land as her own, and in the years that followed, many Russians were involved in exploring the coast and trading with the Alaskan natives. The United States held discussions with Russia about purchasing Alaska as early as 1859, but the deal was put off by the American Civil War. In 1867, the U.S. purchased the Alaskan territory for $7.2 million. The territory became the forty-ninth state in 1959.

   The selection's main pattern of organization is _____
   *(write **list** or **time**).*

(Continues on next page)

7. McDonald's maintains strict and uniform standards of quality through an elaborate management system. First of all, the company runs Hamburger University, a high-power training program for executives and managers of the restaurants. Also, field inspections of food, furnishings and eating areas are frequent and rigorous. Food suppliers who don't meet standards are fired, and managers who don't meet the strictest guidelines for cleanliness are asked to leave.

   The selection's main pattern of organization is _____
   *(write **list** or **time**).*

8. Air-filled tires have several advantages over solid rubber ones, according to the chief engineer for product design at the Akron Technical Center of the Goodyear Tire and Rubber Company. For one thing, air-filled tires, also known as pneumatic tires, are less expensive than solid ones. Also, pneumatic tires are lighter and thus easier to handle than solid tires. Third, the rubber foam that is inside of all-rubber tires quickly builds up heat because of internal friction, causing the foam to melt, but pneumatic tires do not build up such heat. Finally, because pneumatic tires are more yielding, they offer a much smoother ride than solid tires, which make for very bumpy rides.

   The selection's main pattern of organization is _____
   *(write **list** or **time**).*

9. Active listening, or listening at your best, is defined by one of this country's premier listening experts as a four-stage process. Obviously, good listening begins when you sense the speaker's message. Sensing is the process of receiving the speaker's sounds through the auditory system and registering them in the brain. After the message has been sensed, a second stage occurs when you accurately interpret the message or assign meaning to the sounds you receive. Third, if you are listening actively, you evaluate the message by weighing evidence and sorting fact from opinion. To complete the process, you respond by providing feedback or taking action.

   The selection's main pattern of organization is _____
   *(write **list** or **time**).*

10. The word *museum* makes people think of dinosaur skeletons, Egyptian mummies, and ancient cave drawings. But there are less well-known museums available to entertain and educate people of all interests. One such unusual museum is Mont Hollertz Chevyland USA in Elm Creek, Nebraska. More than eighty Chevrolet automobiles, all restored and in running condition, are displayed there. Then there's the Liberace Museum in Las Vegas. Many possessions of the flashy pianist-showman are on exhibit there. They include customized cars, a jeweled miniature piano presented to Liberace by the Queen of England, and Liberace's $60,000 copy of King George V's coronation robe. Yet another off-beat museum is the Red Light Museum in Washington, D.C. This museum serves to house mementoes of the world's oldest profession, prostitution. A nineteenth-century sex manual, a racy Victorian-era slide show, and erotic postcards are among the exhibits there.

   The selection's main pattern of organization is _____
   *(write **list** or **time**).*

Name _____

Section _____ Date _____

SCORE: (Number correct) × 10 = _____%

RELATIONSHIPS II: Test 1

Read each item, and then answer the question about relationships in the space provided. Write in either the transition or the pattern of organization.

1. Crawling babies often try to put in their mouths any object that they find. Therefore, parents should be alert for dangerous items left on floors and carpets.

    The cause and effect transition used is _____ *(write one word).*

2. I think our dog doesn't hear very well anymore. He doesn't bark, for example, when the mail truck stops in front of our house.

    The example transition used is _____ *(write two words).*

3. Just as Mr. Thomas loves tinkering with automobiles, his sons enjoy fixing up old motorcycles.

    The comparison transition used is _____ *(write two words).*

4. Big letters on the box read, "Blueberry Muffins"; however, in small print is written, "Imitation Blueberries."

    The contrast transition used is _____ *(write one word).*

5. My mother is very superstitious. As a result, she never has thirteen people for dinner.

    The cause and effect transition used is _____ *(write three words).*

6. Members of the American Society of Criminology decided not to hold their convention in Miami because the city has too much crime.

    The selection's main pattern of organization is _____
    *(write **def and example**, or **comparison**, or **contrast**, or **cause and effect**).*

7. Name calling is the use of emotionally loaded names, or labels, to turn people against a rival product, candidate, or movement. A politician being called a "wimp" by his opponents is an instance of name calling.

    The selection's main pattern of organization is _____
    *(write **def and example**, or **comparison**, or **contrast**, or **cause and effect**).*

(Continues on next page)

8. Our memories are a lot like funhouse mirrors. When we look into a funhouse mirror, we see ourselves as shorter, taller, thinner, or fatter than we really are. Similarly, we tend to remember events differently from the way they really were.

The selection's main pattern of organization is _____
(write **def and example**, or **comparison**, or **contrast**, or **cause and effect**).

9. The cost of a single-family home has risen tremendously in the last few years. As a result, more and more people are renting instead of buying.

The selection's main pattern of organization is _____
(write **def and example**, or **comparison**, or **contrast**, or **cause and effect**).

10. You can usually see the players' moves better when watching sports on television. On the other hand, you can enjoy more directly the excitement of the crowd when watching in person.

The selection's main pattern of organization is _____
(write **def and example**, or **comparison**, or **contrast**, or **cause and effect**).

TEN STEPS TO IMPROVING
COLLEGE READING SKILLS
Note: This test is identical to the Townsend Press Software Test 2 on Relationships II.

Name _____

Section _____ Date _____

SCORE: (Number correct) × 10 = _____%

RELATIONSHIPS II: Test 2

Read each item, and then answer the question about relationships in the space provided. Write in either the transition or the pattern of organization.

1. Because I won't be home to watch tonight's *Jeopardy*, I'm recording it on my VCR.

   The cause and effect transition used is _____ *(write one word).*

2. Nicotine is now regarded as an addictive drug, just like heroin.

   The comparison transition used is _____ *(write two words).*

3. Some myths are difficult to get rid of. The mistaken idea that ostriches bury their heads in the sand to hide, for instance, has been around for about two thousand years.

   The example transition used is _____ *(write two words).*

4. Even though individuals over 65 make up 11 percent of our population, they buy 25 percent of all prescription drugs sold.

   The contrast transition used is _____ *(write two words).*

5. A tractor-trailer tipped over on the highway during the rain this morning, spilling several cases of detergent. So traffic was held up for hours while the road was cleaned up.

   The cause and effect transition used is _____ *(write one word).*

6. Movie watching is better on cable television than on network TV. Cable viewers get to see the latest box-office hits only months after they play the theaters. And the movies are not edited by network censors. In addition, no commercials interrupt the flow of the action or the mood of the film. In contrast, movies on network TV are often years old. Some of the dialogue may be dubbed to eliminate offensive language. Often, scenes are left out or clumsily edited to tone down violence or sex. And ads constantly interrupt the flow of network movies.

   The selection's main pattern of organization is _____
   *(write **def and example**, or **comparison**, or **contrast**, or **cause and effect**).*

7. A forensic psychologist is a psychologist who interprets professional information for courtroom purposes. At the trial of John Hinckley, Jr., for instance, several forensic psychologists testified about whether or not Hinckley was mentally competent enough to be considered legally responsible for his attempt to assassinate then-President Ronald Reagan.

   The selection's main pattern of organization is _____
   *(write **def and example**, or **comparison**, or **contrast**, or **cause and effect**).*

(Continues on next page)

8. Vietnamese and American cultures are sharply different. In Vietnam, two men or two women often show affection in public, but open affection between the sexes is not considered acceptable. Also, Vietnamese are often surprised by American family relations. Americans may live far from their parents and grandparents. Even if they're in the same city, they rarely live in the same house. However, three or four generations generally live together in one Vietnamese household, with elderly people cared for by their children and grandchildren.

The selection's main pattern of organization is _____
(write **def and example**, *or* **comparison**, *or* **contrast**, *or* **cause and effect**).

9. Habituation is the term for a common behavior pattern: the more we are exposed to something, the less aware we become of it and, therefore, the less we respond to it. During the Vietnam War, reports from the combat zone appeared every night on television. Viewers soon became so used to the news stories that scenes of violence and body counts no longer horrified them. The war became just another television program.

The selection's main pattern of organization is _____
(write **def and example**, *or* **comparison**, *or* **contrast**, *or* **cause and effect**).

10. Black magic and voodoo have many believers among certain parts of the world. There are many stories of a person dying after being the subject of a magical "curse." Scientists find no evidence that such curses have any magical effect. Yet it is undeniable that some cursed people have sickened and died. Researchers studying such cases have found one especially significant element: The cursed people who grew ill knew they had been cursed and deeply believed in the power of the curse. Scientists have concluded that because of this belief, the curse's victims were actually frightened to death. The terror of knowing that one has been cursed could actually trigger a fatal irregular heartbeat.

The selection's main pattern of organization is _____
(write **def and example**, *or* **comparison**, *or* **contrast**, *or* **cause and effect**).

Note: This test is identical to the Townsend Press Software Test 1 on Fact and Opinion.

Name _____

Section _____ Date _____

SCORE: (Number correct) × 10 = _____%

FACT AND OPINION: Test 1

In the space provided, write an **F** if a sentence states a fact. Write an **O** if it expresses an opinion.

_____ 1. During his career, pitcher Bob Miller was traded ten times.

_____ 2. Bob Miller was the worst pitcher ever to play in the major leagues.

_____ 3. A zookeeper at the Houston Zoo was killed by a Siberian tiger.

_____ 4. More than twenty people called the zoo to demand the death of the tiger that killed the zookeeper.

_____ 5. Tigers in zoos should be killed if they behave like wild animals.

_____ 6. Reading assignments for Introduction to Psychology include two textbooks, a biography, and a collection of case studies.

_____ 7. The reading in Introduction to Psychology is too difficult for freshmen.

_____ 8. More schools should recognize the importance of teaching children about their own bodies.

_____ 9. Teaching children about their bodies is part of our required science curriculum.

_____ 10. In fact, our science curriculum is the best in the state.

TEN STEPS TO IMPROVING
COLLEGE READING SKILLS

Note: This test is identical to the Townsend Press Software Test 2 on Fact and Opinion.

Name _____

Section _____ Date _____

SCORE: (Number correct) × 10 = _____%

FACT AND OPINION: Test 2

In the space provided, write an **F** if a sentence states a fact. Write an **O** if it expresses an opinion.

_____ 1. Cicadas, commonly called seventeen-year locusts, hibernate in the ground for seventeen years at a time.

_____ 2. Clearly, cicadas are one of nature's strangest insects.

_____ 3. In Cleveland, two robbers once stole twenty-five dollars from a convenience store after scaring off the cashier with a cicada.

_____ 4. Snakes are far scarier than cicadas.

_____ 5. Certain news magazines publish national and international editions every week.

_____ 6. CNN covers the news more intelligently than other networks do.

_____ 7. There was nothing interesting to watch on television this evening.

_____ 8. The novel *Alice's Adventures in Wonderland* was written by Charles Lutwidge Dodgson under the pen name Lewis Carroll.

_____ 9. *Alice's Adventures in Wonderland* is one of the more charming children's books.

_____ 10. Of all the artists who have illustrated *Alice's Adventures in Wonderland*, none has surpassed Tenniel's enchanting drawings.

TEN STEPS TO IMPROVING
COLLEGE READING SKILLS

Name _____

Section _____ Date _____

Note: This test is identical to the Townsend Press Software Test 1 on Inferences.

SCORE: (Number correct) × 10 = _____%

INFERENCES: Test 1

In the space provided, write the letter of the inference that is most firmly based on the given facts in each selection.

___ 1. A piece of candy had melted on the sidewalk, and dozens of ants were crawling around it.
   A. Ants prefer candy to anything else.
   B. The candy attracted the ants.
   C. Candy attracts many types of insects.

___ 2. Maria looked out of the restaurant window; it was still pouring outside. "I guess it won't matter if I stay here a few more minutes," she thought. "Maybe it will clear up soon." Then she asked the waiter for another cup of coffee.
   A. Maria had an appointment.
   B. Maria hoped the rain would stop soon.
   C. Maria had forgotten her umbrella.

___ 3. Charles read the newspaper very slowly, for he was a poor reader.
   A. Charles was not very bright.
   B. Charles was a high-school dropout.
   C. Charles hadn't learned how to read well.

___ 4. The sloth is a tree-dwelling animal of the American tropics. It eats leaves by inching along a branch in an upside-down position, using its claws as hooks. A sloth spends the vast majority of its time sleeping and resting. Indeed, it moves about so little that green algae—a form of vegetation—actually grows on its fur. Once you understand a little bit about the nature of sloths, it's easy to understand why one of the dictionary definitions of "slothful" is "lazy"!
   A. The sloth probably has strong claws.
   B. The sloth probably has very little fur.
   C. The sloth probably has a huge appetite.

___ 5. Sally and Erica have very different approaches to getting ready for 9 a.m. class. Sally gets up at 7 a.m., takes a shower, dresses, eats breakfast, and reviews her notes before leaving for class. Erica, on the other hand, has her alarm set for 8 a.m., repeatedly hits the "snooze" button on the alarm clock, and finally gets out of bed at 8:45. She dresses in a hurry and runs out the door to class, complaining that she never has enough time in the morning.
   A. Sally and Erica could never be good friends.
   B. Erica will get a poor grade in that class.
   C. Sally is more organized in the mornings than Erica.

(Continues on next page)

_____ 6. Two children were in the living room. One was just a baby who could barely crawl. The other was three years old. There was a series of red crayon lines under the window sill that hadn't been there before. A box of crayons was on the coffee table.
A. The three-year-old made the red crayon marks.
B. The baby pulled himself up and made the marks.
C. The baby made the marks by throwing the crayons.

_____ 7. Cats have gone through many changes of status since they began living with humans thousands of years ago. The ancient Egyptians worshiped them and preserved their bodies as mummies—sometimes providing them with mummified mice to chase in the afterlife. During the Middle Ages, in contrast, cats were the victims of superstition, and thousands were burned as witches' partners. Even the classic cartoons of the 1940s and 1950s often presented cats as the villains. Since then, however, cats have made a comeback. Today, cats are even more popular as pets than dogs.
A. There were no dogs in ancient Egypt.
B. Today, dogs are no longer popular as pets.
C. During the Middle Ages, some people believed in witches.

_____ 8. Harry Shepherd was the computer expert at Hay's Department Store; he had set up and run the store's system from the start. Harry was a warm, friendly man who went out of his way to help fellow workers. In his neighborhood, he was known as a gentle father and someone who contributed a lot to every good cause. One day, he was accused of embezzling thousands of dollars over the last few years. A program on the computer was discovered that shorted a customer by a few cents every time he or she got a refund. Harry's bank account was also found to be much healthier than someone with his income would ordinarily have. Also, he had quite a bit of cash in a safety deposit box at the bank.
A. Harry was probably guilty.
B. Harry was probably innocent.

_____ 9. Throughout history, more than a few famous people were vegetarians. For example, Pythagoras, the famous Greek mathematician who lived in the fifth century B.C., kept to a simple diet of bread, honey, and vegetables. Plato and Aristotle were also vegetarians. The poet Percy Bysshe Shelley became a convert to vegetarianism at twenty-one and later wrote a pamphlet in its defense. And Count Tolstoi, the Russian author famous for *War and Peace*, not only ate no animals; he would eat no eggs.
A. Most authors have been vegetarians.
B. Some vegetarians eat eggs.
C. Most vegetarians are men.

(Continues on next page)

____10. In the mid-1970s the networks tried to break down traditional viewing habits by introducing a new format, the miniseries. The idea was to get people hooked on the series in the first episode—usually broadcast on Sunday night—so they would tune in again the next several evenings. Miniseries have proven very popular, and they are often scheduled during "sweep periods," when TV stations are monitored to determine audience sizes. (Sweeps are usually conducted three times a year—November, February, and May—and are used to set advertising rates. High ratings means higher ad rates for the local stations and networks.)

A. Advertisers probably like miniseries because they are educational.

B. Advertisers probably like miniseries because the networks charge more when miniseries are shown.

C. Advertisers probably like miniseries because their popularity means many people will see the show's ads.

TEN STEPS TO IMPROVING
COLLEGE READING SKILLS

Note: This test is identical to the Townsend Press Software Test 2 on Inferences.

Name _____

Section _____ Date _____

SCORE: (Number correct) × 10 = _____%

INFERENCES: Test 2

Read each passage and then write the letter of the answer to the inference question.

___ 1. Around 1770, William Addis was put in jail for causing a riot. While in prison, he at first brushed his teeth as everyone else did then—he rubbed them with a rag. Addis decided, however, that the method could be improved. So he proceeded to make tiny holes in a small bone he had saved from a meal. Then he got some stiff bristles from a guard. He cut the bristles, tied them in tufts, glued them at one end, and then squeezed the tufts into the holes on the bone.

What had Addis invented?
A. A hair brush
B. A toothbrush
C. Dental floss

___ 2. The typical American breakfast includes eggs fried in butter, toast dripping with butter, and sausage or bacon. But experts say such a high-fat breakfast puts a burden on the digestion system, causing drowsiness. To stay alert all morning, eat instead a low-fat, high-protein breakfast that includes such things as low-fat dairy products and grains.

Which of the following would best follow the passage's recommendation for breakfast?
A. Pancakes made of white flour with a mound of butter and coffee.
B. A sweet roll with one pat of butter and a glass of whole milk.
C. Low-fat yogurt, whole wheat toast with jelly, and a cup of coffee with skim milk in it.

___ 3. Among the numerous heroes of history are animals. One was a canary named Bibs. Bibs was the pet of an elderly woman, Tess, who lived alone in Tennessee. Tess's niece lived nearby. One day the niece heard a tapping at her window and discovered Bibs. The niece quickly went to her aunt's house and found Tess had struck her head on something and fallen over. Bibs died after alerting the niece.

From the paragraph, which of the following can we assume to be true?
A. Bibs knew where the niece lived.
B. Bibs was always kept caged.
C. Bibs was never kept caged.

___ 4. Many interior designers seem to think plastic plants are superior to real ones. Real plants, however, can do much that even the most realistic plastic ones can't. Plants, for instance, improve the quality of the air by giving off oxygen and absorbing certain air pollutants. Also, they cool the air as water evaporates from their leaves. Large plants—trees and shrubs—can even muffle the otherwise harsh sounds of construction work and street traffic.

(Continues on next page)

Based on the evidence in the paragraph, which of the following statements would its author be most likely to agree with?

A. Plastic plants are too expensive.

B. Plastic plants are used too often.

C. Plastic plants are ugly.

_____ 5. Hospices are different from hospitals and nursing homes in a couple of ways. First of all, hospices treat patients suffering from incurable diseases who are not expected to live for more than a year. Hospitals, however, aim to help patients recover from disease, and nursing homes provide long-term care for the handicapped and elderly. Also, the hospice's purpose is to help the dying and their families. In contrast, hospitals and nursing homes have limited resources for helping patients' families.

Where would a person handicapped with constant arthritis who could not care for her- or himself be more likely to go?

A. Hospice

B. Hospital

C. Nursing home

_____ 6. There are a few steps you can take to remember your dreams. First, you must make the decision that you want to remember your dreams, for such a conscious decision makes it more likely to happen. Next, keep a pen and notebook near your bed, so you can write down what you remember as soon as you wake up. Also, when possible, keep your alarm off, for the noise of an alarm can interfere with your memory of your dreams. Finally, when you wake up with the memory of a dream, write it down immediately, even before you get out of bed.

Based on the paragraph, which of the following ways **not** mentioned there would be more likely to be helpful in remembering dreams?

A. Before you go to sleep, try to remember your dreams from the night before.

B. Record on a tape recorder what you remember of your dreams before getting out of bed each morning.

C. Keep a notebook and pen nearby during your work day.

_____ 7. The housemother of a dormitory for student nurses was fired for helping a battered woman because in doing so she broke school rules. According to the dormitory security rules, the housemother cannot let strangers in on her own after the 1 a.m. curfew. Instead, she must first check with the security guard. One night after curfew, a stranger banged on the door. It was a young woman bruised from a beating by her husband, so the housemother let the woman in immediately. Two days later the housemother was fired.

From the paragraph, which of the following can we conclude about the housemother?

A. She felt an exception could be made.

B. She had no regard for the rules.

C. She had made far too many exceptions.

(Continues on next page)

___ 8. Both of Larry's parents worked. One was an accountant, and the other was an interior decorator. Larry had given a lot of thought to his own line of work and finally decided to do exactly what his father did.

Which profession did Larry choose?
A. Accountancy
B. Interior decorating
C. Either accountancy or interior decorating

___ 9. When the Spanish conqueror Pizarro transferred the capital of Peru from a site in the mountains 11,000 feet above sea level to lowland Lima, it wasn't just for a change of scenery. The Spanish conquerors observed early that domestic animals taken to the mountains failed to reproduce. And for over fifty years after the Spanish brought their wives and settled the Andes, no Spanish children were born in any of the higher altitudes. The Indians, however, described by Spanish priests as healthy and vigorous, were fertile in the same climate. The difference was that over the 9,000 years that the Indians had lived in the Andes, they had developed enlarged lungs, a high red-cell count, and lower blood pressure, all of which enabled them to live normal lives at high altitudes.

Which of the following ideas is suggested by the paragraph?
A. The Indians had invited the Spanish to govern Peru.
B. A people's genetic makeup can be gradually changed by the environment.
C. The Spaniards were used to living in the mountains.

___ 10. A theory suggests that the dinosaurs might have been killed off by a comet that struck Earth millions of years ago. The impact produced a huge cloud that covered Earth's surface and blocked off sunlight—and its beneficial effects on plants and animals—for months or years. This theory was first inspired by a study of giant dust storms on the planet Mars.

Which of the following explanations is suggested by the paragraph for why a huge cloud is thought to be capable of killing off the dinosaurs?
A. The cloud would have made it too dark out for the dinosaurs to hunt.
B. The cloud could have contained poison.
C. By blocking sunlight for so long, the cloud would have killed many of the plants and animals eaten by dinosaurs.

TEN STEPS TO IMPROVING
COLLEGE READING SKILLS

Name _____

Section _____ Date _____

Note: This test is identical to the Townsend Press Software Test 1 on Purpose and Tone.

SCORE: (Number correct) × 10 = _____%

PURPOSE AND TONE: Test 1

In the space provided, indicate whether the primary purpose of each sentence is to inform (**I**), to persuade (**P**), or to entertain (**E**).

_____   1. Given all the injuries that occur, boxing is a sport that should be banned.

_____   2. Soils can be classified in various ways, including according to color, texture, and the type of crops they support.

_____   3. With funerals so expensive, I'd better not die soon; I can't afford to.

_____   4. Thomas Jefferson promised his wife he would never remarry; she died at thirty-three, and he kept his promise.

_____   5. Teachers should not grade on a curve because then no matter how well the poorest student does, he or she cannot get a good grade.

_____   6. The sign in the diner read, "Don't make fun of our coffee. You too may be weak and old some day."

_____   7. July is Bargain Month at Fred's Used Cars and Trucks. Now's your chance to make a real deal and drive away with the car of your dreams.

_____   8. March 1 is the deadline for all applications for scholarships and student loans.

_____   9. The spaceship landed. Stella's heart pounded as two aliens stepped out. Would Jeffrey be in there, and alive?

_____   10. Unless citizens work together to stop developers from turning parkland into parking lots, our children won't recognize a tree or a blade of grass.

TEN STEPS TO IMPROVING
COLLEGE READING SKILLS

Name _____

Section _____ Date _____

*Note: This test is identical to the Townsend Press Software Test 2
on Purpose and Tone.*

SCORE: (Number correct) × 10 = _____%

PURPOSE AND TONE: Test 2

In the space provided, write the letter of the word that expresses the tone present in each passage.

___ 1. I always seem to be missing out on things. This time, I'm missing an afternoon at the beach. My boyfriend and some others are driving out to the shore, but I have to stay home and study for finals. Some people have all the luck.
A. sorrowful self-pitying
B. mocking
C. self-pitying

___ 2. George and Martha Washington never had children of their own, but Martha had two children from a previous marriage. Also, after her son Jacky died at the age of twenty-seven, George and Martha adopted two of his children.
A. critical
B. objective
C. loving

___ 3. The people in the apartment across the hallway are good communicators. When they have a party, they communicate it to us by turning the music up so loud that we can't hear our own TV. And when they have an argument, they let us know about that too, by yelling at the top of their lungs.
A. straightforward
B. sarcastic
C. cruel

___ 4. I've sent out dozens of résumés and gone on exactly ten interviews, and I still haven't gotten a job offer. But now I have two more job interviews set up, and I have a feeling in my bones that one of these is going to be a winner.
A. optimistic
B. amused
C. regretful

___ 5. Ladies and gentlemen, I beg of you not to abandon those unfortunate Americans who, through no fault of their own, have lost their homes. These are people who not only need our help; they deserve it. With a little assistance, many homeless people can rebuild their lives and regain their dignity.
A. admiring
B. critical
C. impassioned

(Continues on next page)

___ 6. Benjamin Franklin was a most unusual man. He contributed greatly to society in widely different ways. For example, he began the first free circulating library, successfully worked with the British for the repeal of the Stamp Act, and invented bifocals and the Franklin stove.
A. compassionate
B. admiring
C. joyous

___ 7. Hi there, sports fans. This is Hank McGee, coming to you from radio station WSPT, first with the latest in sports news from around the nation. And today we're live in the locker room of the Outlaws, the hottest team in the Eastern League. Let's listen up, folks, while the Outlaws' head honcho tells just how he got his guys back in the win column.
A. insulting
B. informal
C. serious

___ 8. How could our own children have forgotten our anniversary? I don't even care if they don't give us a present, but they could at least have called and wished us a happy anniversary. They always seem to remember to call us when they need money or a babysitter.
A. complaining
B. revengeful
C. tolerant

___ 9. We are gathered here today to remember our friend and neighbor, Lonnie Bartram, and to share in the grief of his sorrowing family. For sixty years, Lonnie lived among us as a loving husband, a caring and affectionate father, a diligent worker, and a friend who could be counted on. He set an example for us all, and we are better men and women for having known him.
A. angry
B. forgiving
C. solemn

___ 10. To connect a videocassette recorder to your television set, you must place the VCR between your antenna or cable connection and the set itself. First, disconnect the VHF or cable antenna input from the TV terminals and connect it to the rear panel of the VCR. Then run another cable from the VHF OUT terminal of the VCR directly to the television set.
A. matter-of-fact
B. tolerant
C. light-hearted

TEN STEPS TO IMPROVING
COLLEGE READING SKILLS

Name _____

Section _____ Date _____

Note: This test is identical to the Townsend Press Software Test 1 on Argument.

SCORE: (Number correct) × 10 = _____%

ARGUMENT: Test 1

One statement in each group is the point of an argument. The other statements are support for that point. Write the letter of the statement that is the point of each argument.

____ 1. A. My English final is tomorrow morning.
B. I'd better stay home and study tonight.

____ 2. A. You can relax and watch the scenery by train.
B. The best way to travel is by train.
C. On a train, you can easily get up and move around.

____ 3. A. That dog is unfriendly.
B. That dog growls at anyone who tries to pet it.
C. That dog snarls and hides under the sofa when there's company.

____ 4. A. My school expenses, insurance, gas, and room-and-board payments to my parents amount to $190 a month.
B. Since my hours were cut, I earn $100 a week as a dishwasher.
C. I need a higher-paying job.

____ 5. A. Being a doctor is a high-stress, demanding profession.
B. A doctor's mistake can result in the loss of a patient's life.
C. Doctors must keep up with all current research in their field.

____ 6. A. A free, nutritional breakfast should be available to all students.
B. Students who eat breakfast are more alert during morning classes.
C. Some students don't get sufficient nutrition at home.

____ 7. A. That street is poorly lit at night.
B. People shouldn't walk on that street alone at night.
C. Several people have been attacked on that street at night.

____ 8. A. Harvey's desk is always littered with used paper coffee cups and candy wrappers.
B. Obviously, Harvey is a slob.
C. There are empty beer cans and peanut shells under Harvey's sofa.

____ 9. A. Esther just opened a new savings account so she could get a free alarm clock.
B. Esther buys gas at a station that gives away cups with each fill-up.
C. It seems Esther can't resist getting something for nothing.
D. Esther loves going to stores on their "grand opening" days, so she can pick up the free souvenirs that merchants give away.

____ 10. A. Lord Austin's study window was open when the body was discovered.
B. The handle of a large bread knife could be seen sticking out of Lord Austin's chest.
C. Someone stabbed Lord Austin and then escaped through the study window.
D. A trail of bloodstained footprints led from Lord Austin's body to the window of his study.

TEN STEPS TO IMPROVING
COLLEGE READING SKILLS

Note: This test is identical to the Townsend Press Software Test 2 on Argument.

Name _____

Section _____ Date _____

SCORE: (Number correct) × 10 = _____%

ARGUMENT: Test 2

In the space provided, write the number of the sentence in each paragraph that does not support the conclusion of the argument.

_____ 1. ¹Whenever she has the time, Marie loves to cook. ²On weekends, she cooks half the meals for the coming week. ³She often puts a dessert in the oven just as the family sits down for dinner. ⁴Sometimes instead of cooking, Marie will curl up with a good book.

Which of the above sentences does not contribute to the author's conclusion that Marie loves to cook whenever she has time?

_____ 2. ¹When it comes to his car, Jimmy is overly fussy. ²He washes it every day, even if it's raining. ³He won't even let people in the car unless they've wiped off their shoes. ⁴Yet he exposes the car—and himself—to risk by drag racing on narrow streets. ⁵Once when his girlfriend ate a Danish in the car on the way to school, he later made her vacuum the floor to remove the few crumbs she had dropped.

Which of the above sentences does not support the author's conclusion that Jimmy is overly fussy about his car?

_____ 3. ¹Many short-sighted young people today place too high a value on immediate pleasures. ²They cut back on schoolwork in order to work many hours at part-time jobs so they can afford the latest fashions. ³And they don't even do those jobs all that well, treating customers and bosses alike with disrespect. ⁴Patience and planning have been replaced by such satisfactions as cars and gold chains. ⁵They'd rather wear hundred-dollar tennis shoes than prepare themselves to earn thousands of dollars at a future career.

Which of the above sentences does not contribute to the author's conclusion that many young people today place too high a value on immediate pleasures?

_____ 4. ¹Cindy is a dangerous driver. ²For example, she will often drink and drive. ³Last night she had so much to drink that she had to call her boyfriend to drive her home instead of driving home herself. ⁴Cindy also drives too fast. ⁵She's been given five speeding tickets in the last year and a half.

Which of the above sentences does not contribute to the author's conclusion that Cindy is a dangerous driver?

(Continues on next page)

_____ 5. [1]A cat is often a better choice for a pet than a dog. [2]First of all, cats are better for families who live in apartments. [3]Among the problems of keeping a dog in an apartment is that its barking can disturb other tenants; a cat is relatively quiet. [4]Also, cats require less care and attention than dogs. [5]Finally, it is easy to adopt a cat or kitten from the pound for very little money.

Which of the above sentences does not contribute to the author's conclusion that cats today make better pets than dogs?

_____ 6. [1]Now, listen, Dino, I think you'd better either quit your job or cut back your hours. [2]Your grades have come down ever since you began work. [3]In addition, you never have time to help around the house or help your brother with his homework. [4]Even before you started working, you could have been more helpful to your brother, who, after all, has done many favors for you.

Which of the above sentences does not contribute to the speaker's conclusion that Dino should quit his job or cut back on his hours?

_____ 7. [1]Children's names can have far-reaching effects on them, according to scientists. [2]Some researchers have found that there is a tendency for children with popular names, such as Jennifer or Robert, to be more confident. [3]Such children are also better liked than children with names that are considered undesirable. [4]Some parents insist on naming their children old-fashioned names.

Which of the above sentences does not contribute to the author's conclusion that children's names can have far-reaching effects on them?

_____ 8. [1]All public libraries should hold regular "amnesty days," which are days on which overdue books may be returned without paying a fine. [2]When one community library had an amnesty week, over 2,500 books that might otherwise have not been returned were turned in. [3]One of these books had been kept out for fifteen years, so it is safe to assume the borrower would not have returned the book if a fine had to be paid. [4]But amnesty days aren't exactly fair to those library patrons who return their books on time or pay their fines.

Which of the above sentences does not contribute to the author's conclusion that public libraries should have amnesty days?

(Continues on next page)

_____ 9. [1]You should pay your income taxes honestly and on time. [2]First of all, there is a penalty for filing late. [3]And if you are caught cheating on your taxes, you could be sent to jail. [4]Not enough tax cheaters are sent to jail, which encourages others to continue to cheat on their taxes. [5]Finally, it is your responsibility as a citizen to support the government, its services, and its poor by paying your fair share of taxes.

Which of the above sentences does not contribute to the author's conclusion that you should pay your income taxes honestly and on time?

_____ 10. [1]Animal-rights activists should leave the rest of us in peace. [2]Most fur products are made from animals bred for that purpose. [3]Few endangered species are threatened by the fur industry. [4]Animal-rights activists would even disrupt medical experiments that use lab animals as subjects. [5]They don't realize the importance of testing drugs on live animals before we can benefit from the treatments being developed. [6]They should turn their attention to really important issues such as child abuse. [7]Many drugs that are saving lives today would not have been developed without research on animals.

Which of the above sentences does not support the argument that the use of animals for fur and medical experiments is justified?

TEN STEPS TO IMPROVING
COLLEGE READING SKILLS

*Note: This test is identical to the Townsend Press Software Test 1
on Combined Skills.*

Name _____

Section _____ Date _____

SCORE: (Number correct) × 10 = _____%

COMBINED SKILLS: Test 1

After reading the textbook passage, write the letter of the best answer to each question.

[1]We tend to think that children in the same family will grow up to be more similar than unrelated people. [2]This is a fundamental part of our lore: brothers who are alike in their enjoyment of sports or sisters who both take up the law. [3]However, comprehensive studies in Sweden, Great Britain, the United States, Finland, and other countries show that a shared family environment does not affect children's personalities at all! [4]This is because, even within a family, each child grows up in a thoroughly different world from the others.

[5]Although siblings share many genes, other factors, including birth order, make children live in distinct worlds and develop quite differently even in the same home. [6]The research leads to a radical conclusion: families do not make us similar to our siblings; they make us different. [7]Genetics accounts for similarities among children in the same families, but it is family experiences that make them different. [8]Most parents, for instance, treat girls differently from boys and firstborns differently from those born later.

[9]For example, two sisters were at a dinner party when the conversation turned to upbringing. [10]The elder sister started to say that her parents had been very strict and that she had been rather frightened of them. [11]Her sister, younger by two years, interrupted in amazement. [12]"What are you talking about?" she said. [13]"Our parents were very lenient. [14]I remember being allowed to stay out late and to do all sorts of things. [15]How could you call them strict?"

[16]Both were accurate: one sister had received different treatment from the other. [17]The first child had borne the brunt of parental anxiety all through her childhood and was stopped from doing things that might possibly be dangerous or unsuitable. [18]But by the time the young one was growing up, the parents had learned to relax a bit, since the first daughter hadn't gotten into trouble, and they were much more likely to let the second daughter do what she wanted.

[19]Although certain personality traits do run in families, siblings are far more disparate than they are alike. [20]When they are tested, their scores are as different as those of unrelated people brought up separately.

____ 1. In sentence 5, the word *siblings* means
   A. brothers.
   B. sisters.
   C. brothers or sisters.
   D. friends.

____ 2. In sentence 19, the word *disparate* means
   A. different.
   B. equal.
   C. well-known.
   D. unknown.

(Continues on next page)

_____ 3. According to the author, children in the same family
   A. share few genes.
   B. are brought up similarly.
   C. receive different parental treatment.
   D. do not get along as adults.

_____ 4. The author implies that
   A. most parents do a poor job of bringing up their children.
   B. parents should treat all of their children exactly the same.
   C. many people believe brothers and sisters are more alike than they really are.
   D. genes account for the majority of our characteristics.

_____ 5. The relationship of the third and fourth paragraphs to the previous paragraphs is one of
   A. addition.
   B. time.
   C. illustration.
   D. comparison.

_____ 6. The relationship between the two parts of sentence 19 is one of
   A. time.
   B. comparison.
   C. contrast.
   D. cause and effect.

_____ 7. The main pattern of organization of the fourth paragraph is
   A. list of items.
   B. time order.
   C. contrast.
   D. definition and example.

_____ 8. The author's main purpose is to
   A. inform readers about brothers and sisters.
   B. persuade readers to bring up their children more consistently.
   C. entertain readers with humorous family stories.

_____ 9. Which is the most appropriate title for this selection?
   A. Testing Siblings
   B. Shared Genes, Shared Upbringing
   C. Parental Anxiety About Bringing Up Children
   D. The Same Parents But Different Upbringings

_____ 10. Which sentence best expresses the main idea of the passage?
   A. Sentence 1
   B. Sentence 7
   C. Sentence 8
   D. Sentence 20

TEN STEPS TO IMPROVING
COLLEGE READING SKILLS

Name _____

Section _____ Date _____

Note: This test is identical to the Townsend Press Software Test 2 on Combined Skills.

SCORE: (Number correct) × 10 = _____%

COMBINED SKILLS: Test 2

After reading the textbook passage, write the letter of the best answer to each question.

[1]Do you grab a candy bar when you feel tired? [2]Do you soothe your weary mind with a doughnut? [3]These quick fixes offer a temporary high that could actually be fueling your fatigue, sending you on a blood-sugar roller coaster. [4]For example, researchers at Kansas State University measured mood in 120 college women who drank twelve ounces of water or beverages sweetened with either aspartame (NutraSweet) or sugar. [5]Within thirty minutes the women who drank the sugar-sweetened beverage were the drowsiest. [6]Some people are so sensitive to sugar or caffeine that they feel tired, irritable, or depressed within an hour of eating even two cookies or drinking one cup of coffee. [7]Others can tolerate larger sugar doses before symptoms develop.

[8]Sugar is a good source of carbohydrate—the energy fuel—so why do sweets bring you down? [9]For one thing, unlike starch, which slowly releases carbohydrate units called glucose into the blood, sugar dumps rapidly into the bloodstream, causing a rapid rise in blood sugar. [10]To counteract this rise, the pancreas quickly releases insulin, which shuttles excess sugar from the blood into the cells. [11]Consequently blood sugar drops, often to levels lower than before the snack.

[12]Sugar also increases tryptophan levels in the brain and triggers the release of the brain chemical serotonin, which in turn slows you down. [13]A researcher and a professor of psychology at the Massachusetts Institute of Technology report that people feel sleepier and have "less vigor" for up to three and a half hours after eating a highly refined carbohydrate snack, as compared to a snack that contains more protein.

[14]Finally, people who frequently snack on sweets are likely to consume inadequate amounts of the energizing nutrients. [15]Researchers in Australia report that the more sugar people consume, the higher their fat and calorie consumption and the lower their intake of vitamins and minerals.

[16]Consuming sugar as a quick fix for dwindling energy merely results in a temporary high, but in the long run, it can initiate a vicious energy cycle.

____ 1. In the last sentence, the word *initiate* means
    A. block.
    B. begin.
    C. follow.
    D. disturb.

____ 2. Excess sugar is brought from the blood into the cells by
    A. caffeine.
    B. carbohydrates.
    C. glucose.
    D. insulin.

(Continues on next page)

_____ 3. Sugar increases the release of
   A. insulin.
   B. tryptophan.
   C. serotonin.
   D. all of the above.

_____ 4. Excess sugar intake eventually slows the body down by
   A. leading to a rapid decrease of blood sugar.
   B. leading to the release of serotonin, a brain chemical that slows us down.
   C. contributing to a diet with inadequate amounts of energizing nutrients.
   D. all of the above.

_____ 5. The main pattern of organization of the whole selection is
   A. comparison and/or contrast.
   B. time order.
   C. definition and example.
   D. cause and effect.

_____ 6. We can conclude that a quick energy boost results when sugar
   A. increases tryptophan levels.
   B. is moved into the cells.
   C. rapidly pours into the bloodstream.
   D. works together with starch.

_____ 7. The passage suggests that a high-protein snack
   A. is similar to a highly refined carbohydrate snack.
   B. should be eaten with carbohydrates.
   C. provides more long-term energy than a high-sugar snack.
   D. contains more fat and calories than a sugary snack.

_____ 8. Sentence 4 is
   A. fact.
   B. opinion.

_____ 9. The main idea of sentences 8–15 is that
   A. sugar is a good source of carbohydrates.
   B. there are a few reasons why sugar slows us down.
   C. sugar has several interesting effects on the body.
   D. eating a moderate amount of sweets may be okay for some people.

_____ 10. Which sentence best expresses the central point of this selection?
   A. Sentence 6
   B. Sentence 8
   C. Sentence 14
   D. Sentence 16

ANSWERS TO THE TESTS IN THE SECOND TEST BANK

VOCABULARY IN CONTEXT: Test 1

1. A
2. C
3. B
4. C
5. B
6. B
7. C
8. A
9. B
10. B

VOCABULARY IN CONTEXT: Test 2

1. A
2. C
3. B
4. C
5. B
6. C
7. A
8. B
9. C
10. B

MAIN IDEAS: Test 1

1. B
2. C
3. A
4. C
5. B
6. A
7. B
8. C
9. B
10. B

MAIN IDEAS: Test 2

1. 8
2. 2
3. 3
4. 1
5. 1
6. 3
7. 2
8. 1
9. 5
10. 2

SUPPORTING DETAILS: Test 1

1. A
2. B
3. B
4. C
5. B
6. C
7. C
8. A
9. B
10. C

SUPPORTING DETAILS: Test 2

1. C
2. C
3. C
4. B
5. C
6. B
7. C
8. B
9. A
10. C

IMPLIED MAIN IDEAS/CENTRAL POINT: Test 1

1. B
2. C
3. C
4. A
5. C
6. B
7. B
8. B
9. C
10. A

IMPLIED MAIN IDEAS/CENTRAL POINT: Test 2

1. 2
2. 1
3. 22
4. 1
5. 3
6. 4
7. 1
8. 15
9. 5
10. 4

RELATIONSHIPS I: Test 1

1. Furthermore
2. After
3. Also
4. When
5. In addition
6. time
7. list
8. list
9. time
10. time

RELATIONSHIPS I: Test 2

1. Next
2. also
3. Finally
4. second
5. When
6. time
7. list
8. list
9. time
10. list

RELATIONSHIPS II: Test 1

1. Therefore
2. for example
3. Just as
4. however
5. As a result
6. cause and effect
7. def and example
8. comparison
9. cause and effect
10. contrast

RELATIONSHIPS II: Test 2

1. Because
2. just like
3. for instance
4. Even though
5. So
6. contrast
7. def and example
8. contrast
9. def and example
10. cause and effect

FACT AND OPINION: Test 1

1. F		6. F	
2. O		7. O	
3. F		8. O	
4. F		9. F	
5. O		10. O	

INFERENCES: Test 1

1. B		6. A	
2. B		7. C	
3. C		8. A	
4. A		9. B	
5. C		10. C	

PURPOSE AND TONE: Test 1

1. P		6. E	
2. I		7. P	
3. E		8. I	
4. I		9. E	
5. P		10. P	

ARGUMENT: Test 1

1. B		6. A	
2. B		7. B	
3. A		8. B	
4. C		9. C	
5. A		10. C	

COMBINED SKILLS: Test 1

1. C		6. C	
2. A		7. C	
3. C		8. A	
4. C		9. D	
5. C		10. B	

FACT AND OPINION: Test 2

1. F		6. O	
2. O		7. O	
3. F		8. F	
4. O		9. O	
5. F		10. O	

INFERENCES: Test 2

1. B		6. B	
2. C		7. A	
3. A		8. C	
4. B		9. B	
5. C		10. C	

PURPOSE AND TONE: Test 2

1. C		6. B	
2. B		7. B	
3. B		8. A	
4. A		9. C	
5. C		10. A	

ARGUMENT: Test 2

1. 4		6. 4	
2. 4		7. 4	
3. 3		8. 4	
4. 3		9. 4	
5. 5		10. 6	

COMBINED SKILLS: Test 2

1. B		6. C	
2. D		7. C	
3. D		8. A	
4. D		9. B	
5. D		10. D	

Notes